basic Fly Fishing
& Fly Tying

basic
Fly Fishing
& Fly Tying

RAY OVINGTON

Stackpole Books

BASIC FLY FISHING AND FLY TYING

Copyright © 1973 by
The Stackpole Company

Published by
STACKPOLE BOOKS
Cameron and Kelker Streets
Harrisburg, Pa. 17105

Printed in the U.S.A.

Library of Congress Cataloging in Publication Data

Ovington, Ray.
  Basic fly fishing and fly tying.

  Includes bibliographical references.
    1. Fly fishing. 2. Fly tying. I. Title.
SH456.O88   799.1'2   73-12849
ISBN 0-8117-0200-6
ISBN 0-8117-2013-6 (pbk.)

Contents

Preface

RAY OVINGTON HAS come forth with a book that in my opinion fulfills a great need; a book simply written and plainly illustrated which covers the tackle, gear, casting, fishing and fly tying and general needed lore—all in one small, inexpensive book.

Look at the books that are available and you'll find that they are excellent, true, but the more expensive and extensive are far too much for the beginner or—at the other extreme—too general, too short and not detailed enough for the angler to really get his teeth into the subject and be able to become a good fisherman.

Ray has written the more detailed and extensive books before, and when I suggested that he write a book of this sort he began adding too much text which would end up in another large tome, not the book that I felt was needed. So I went to work on him with shears and tightened pen and this is the result.

9

It should and will become, I feel, a standard text for the teaching of the art of fly fishing in fresh and salt water and in fly tying. Anyone wishing to go further into details and more lore is invited to peruse the list of titles listed for additional reading at the end of this book. But if the reader of this volume never reads another book on fly fishing he will have read enough to put him on the water, well equipped and well schooled, if he follows Ray's directions. He'll be a good angler and will catch fish. That's the point of the project.

Duncan Cambell
Youth Program Chairman
Federation of Fly
Fishermen
Orange, California

Foreword

RAY OVINGTON IS a friend of mine. He is also a fishing pal and I think he paints a pretty good fish picture, particularly trout. Two of his beautiful paintings decorate my walls and their reality helps me over the long winter evenings when there is very little "running water" fishing, and, oh yes, Ray also writes books; but more on that later. Another thing. He is a fine after dinner speaker. He can show his listeners a lot about the stream and how to go about fishing it. He's been tying flies for a long time and knows almost all there is to the tricks to fly tying.

BASIC FLY FISHING AND FLY TYING was developed under the watchful eyes of several of the members of Orange County Fly Fishers Club, in California, an early member of the Federation of Fly Fishers. Many of the members have gotten to know Ray and to appreciate his know-how and angling savvy. This book of his is basic. I recommend it because it is simple and direct. He writes it and illustrates it in a step-by-step manner. Everything that is necessary to become a fly fisherman is carefully explained. The book also encourages a new fisher to delve deeper into both the arts and sciences of fly fishing not only in "running waters" but also in casting the fly in salt water. He has contributed much to the basic FFF concepts of conserving our natural heritage of "Cleaner Waters, and Brighter Streams".

You will enjoy his book.

Mark Kerridge
Orange County Fly Fishers
VP, Federation of Fly Fishermen
Fullerton, California

Acknowledgments

MY SPECIAL THANKS are due Mark Kerridge, Vice President of the Federation of Fly Fishermen for his astute knowledge and experience and the use of his extensive angling library, donated by him to the California State University at Fullerton, California. I am also grateful to Duncan Cambell, Chairman of the Youth Committee of FFF for his invaluable assistance in preparation of the manuscript and drawings.

R.O.

Introduction

IT IS A pleasure to offer this book to all those—young and old, expert and novice—who desire to learn or refresh their techniques to gain more fun fishing with artificial flies, whether in a small brook, a wide lake or the unlimited ocean.

Fly fishing is only one of the several types of angling requiring its special tackle and techniques. Like the other forms of fishing such as spinning, bait casting and trolling, it can be undertaken and appreciated as an art and enjoyed as such or it can merely be regarded as just another means to an end—catching fish. It is hoped that the reader will discover the art in it, experience the grace that comes in using a finely made fly rod, and enjoy the ultimate of thrills in playing and landing the great variety of sport and food fish to be found in America. As the fisherman becomes experienced, his respect and love of Nature's bounties will grow. Then, as is so often the case, he may devote much time and energy to the protection of the natural resources that provide his angling sport and recreation. He'll also help spread the gospel of sportsmanship and conservation throughout the land, especially to the younger generation who will, it is hoped, develop many true sportsmen—like father, like son—to continue the fine art of fly fishing and promote the protection and development of tomorrow's good fishing waters.

In this book the basics on selecting tackle and accessories are covered early; this is followed by instruction on casting with a fly rod, usually the fisherman's biggest stumbling block to fly rod use. The various fly fishing methods are covered next—dry fly vs. wet fly fishing are treated separately, but the text also covers bass fishing and saltwater fly fishing.

Fishing methods vary somewhat as the season progresses; the text covers it all—from Opening Day and early season techniques to night fishing and late season fishing. Since not all fly fishermen are necessarily trout fishermen there is a special chapter on fishing lakes and artificial impoundments. The chapter on fly tying, which follows, covers the tools and materials needed and explains how to tie most of the proven flies, streamers and bucktails. Of much importance to those who will wish to do some fly tying are the illustrations in this chapter which clarify the various tying steps.

The remainder of the book covers some topics so often overlooked in other fishing books; one is on setting up and planning a fishing trip, another tells how fishing tackle was developed and improved in America and then also reviews most of the important literature that has been produced on fly fishing since the sport's beginnings.

The book concludes with notes on conservation and interesting information on how the Federation of Fly Fishermen came into being and its place in today's efforts for better conservation and angling.

A basic book on fly fishing such as this is meant to be just that. The additional suggested readings listed at the end of the book are for those who may want to broaden their knowledge of the history, lore, mechanics and art of fly fishing. In any event, I believe the beginning fly fisherman who studies this book and follows its suggestions on tackle and other equipment, the techniques for fly fishing in various situations and the tips on best places to cast as indicated in many of the drawings will find his efforts well rewarded.

R.O.

1

~~~~~~

Why Fly
Fishing?

THE MERE FACT that this book is in your hands is enough justification and answer to the chief question raised in this chapter. You want to try it, whether you have yet to fish in any form or manner or if you, like millions of anglers, have caught fish with bait, on spinning gear, bait-casting outfits or a cane pole or even by plain hand line.

It can be your first experience in fishing and perhaps your last, or maybe the end of a long trail of experiments with fishing methods.

FLY FISHING'S NOT JUST FOR TROUT

The "why" of fly fishing means many things to many people. To the purist, brought up in the school of the art in which it is taught that all other forms of angling are of lesser quality, the fly fisherman tends to be dogmatic about his sport. Even among these fly fishermen, there are the specialists and ultra-purists—those dry fly fishermen who look down their noses at wet fly and nymph fishermen, although this is an uncommon extreme. Those who fish with the barbless hook, regardless of whether the fly is dry, wet, nymph or streamer, are another splinter group.

Most of these classes of angler have been exposed to and involved mostly with trout and Atlantic salmon. This heritage comes from Europe, mainly from England where long ago the available fishing became scarce and became limited to a few gentlemen of the art who devised the fly and encouraged its lore as a specialized form of angling aside and apart from general fishing. They called themselves *anglers*, not fishermen. This tradition was imported to America a hundred years ago or so and persists among but a relative few today. The ranks of strict fly fishermen, however, are growing into an unheard of number of anglers who, like their forefathers, have come to realize that fly fishing *is* something different from all other forms of angling.

They see the amount of fishable waters diminishing and the numbers of anglers increasing and, in this bind of supply and demand, are rightly fostering the art of angling with the fly. To justify their claims, they seek to foster the idea that fly fishing for trout and Atlantic salmon is the absolute epitome of the sport of fishing. Their motive is to save the existing streams and return to them most if not all of the fish caught unless they are planted hatchery trout rather than genuine stream-bred, native "wild" trout.

There is not lacking in bait fishing or lure fishing, of course, the need for knowledge, technique and style, but fly fishing—with its imitations of natural insects, baitfish and other foods—is often represented as the most sporting and intriguing way of fishing. And there's a lot to this.

In bass, pike, musky and panfishing, the same restrictions and problems that plague trout fishing as to remaining fishable waters is not so great. Fish other than trout can survive warmer temperatures, some pollution and they are available in many more kinds of water than stream trout, for they are found in broad rivers, lakes and impoundments. Trout, however, are seriously threatened by over-fishing, pollution and a growing lack of streams due to dams, and irrigation. The other species are yet far from troubled by these difficulties. In many cases, they have even increased— benefiting from man's better management and use of their waters. In the ocean and with the exception of salmon there seems to be an unlimited supply of fish of just about all varieties and fishing limits there seem not in the books.

The specialist fly fisherman and purist trout and Atlantic salmon angler have also fished for other freshwater fish such as the black bass with artificial flies instead of bait or lures, simply because of the love of the fly rod and the flies specially designed for these species. And, they've ventured into the salt water, developing a cult of fly fishermen on both coasts who prefer the fly rod and flies to any other method or fishing practice.

On the other hand, there is no such thing as a purist bait fisherman. He fishes with bait because he likes it and is successful, not because of any emotional involvement with the sporting qualities of his method nor particularly for conservation reasons. He doesn't believe in "doing it the hard way" as some bait fishermen might look upon the methods and equipment of the fly fisherman. Nor is the spin fisherman really as much addicted to spinning with the same fervor or rationale as fly fishermen usually are to their sport. He believes that there is much demanding technique and art to successful spinning, but he also knows that spinning gear—even for trout fishing—has its place and capabilities which cannot be duplicated with the fly rod.

But the fly fisherman fishing for trout is usually a whole breed apart, and so is his brother who fishes with similar equipment for other freshwater species or saltwater varieties with the fly rod and artificial-flies-only. All too often he's definitely addicted to his specialty to the point of scorning all other methods. And there are some valid reasons for his attitude, as will be discovered when the art is learned and becomes fully appreciated!

In the case of trout fishing, many believe that eventually, if we are to have any decent trout fishing left in our remaining streams, fishing for them will have to be restricted to fly-fishing-only with no-fish or few-fish limits, or else the fishing may have to be limited to catching and keeping only a few from private or leased waters. The present "open" waters—stocked by the states and left open to all fishing methods—will deteriorate to put-and-take hatchery fish, a far cry from the wild trout fishing that still exists in many places today. Then the concept of the man being able to go out and "catch a mess of trout" will be long gone, unless one wants fresh hatchery deliveries every day and trout that haven't had the time to learn to feed on anything other than hatchery pellets.

FLY FISHING AS AN ART

Why fly fishing? Because it is an art—the highest development of sport fishing methods yet devised. It gives the fish the most sporting chance to size up an offering, as opposed to bait fishing, and the gear needed to float a size 22 dry fly over a four-pound fish is much, much lighter and more fragile or sporting than a ten-pound leader dangling a nightcrawler or minnow before the same fish.

But, from all this, don't get the idea that fly fishing is any less profitable or productive than the other methods. It's as potent a fishing method as the others and in many situations, even much more potent!

Trout feeding on floating insects are comparatively easy game for the dry fly man, while a bait fisherman might not be able to catch a single trout at that same time.

But the moments of striking, playing and landing that trout on a tiny fly and a gossamer thin leader are thrilling moments, far more exciting than hooking that same trout on a worm. The art of delivering the fly, particularly one that you've tied yourself, to that trout or bass or bonefish and fooling him is a plus in pleasure that the average bait fisherman never experiences. The fly man causes the fish to *rise*. The bait or lure fisherman merely waits for something to happen. These are some of the reasons why fly fishing is the art that was and is—and will be. Only after the chips are in and a few years' experience are behind the angler who takes up fly fishing can the dyed-in-the-wool fly fisherman's attitudes and opinions be understood. Try it, you'll like it!

2

~~~~~~

Selecting the Tackle

IMAGINE FOR A moment that an angler is wading hip-deep in the center of a wide stream. The hour is twilight, the currents of the stream divide above the angler because of two big rocks in the center. The angler is fishing upstream to the wash behind these rocks. His long and graceful casts are going out rhythmically forward and backward—false casts—as he wades slowly to a position where he can drop the fly between the washes of the twin rocks. The line stripped from the reel on each false cast lengthens the line in the air, the timing of the forward and backward push of the rod is slower on each addition of line in the air until the angler has decided that he has enough line out to drop the delicate and tiny dry fly right in the riffle. One forward cast puts the fly right over the target and the fly is dropped daintily on the surface. As the angler begins to retrieve the slack line, the fly cocks its wings

and drifts at the mercy of the current, just like a live insect. There
is a splash beneath the fly. The angler, automatically tuned to the
possibility of a strike at any time, quickly hauls back on the line.
His rod bends from the weight of a good fish and its initial spurt
of take-off and run. The ensuing battle is a symphony of careful,
yet relaxed tension of give and take, with the rod being the cushion to apply pressure to the fish and to absorb the quick runs and
jabs of the trout as it fights to escape. That's fly fishing at its
best!

Or, watch a bonefish angler casting a much bigger and more
powerful rod, a long line and leader and a bucktail fly over the gin-
clear Bahama flats. He's spotted a school of bonefish in the lazy
current of a tidal flat. Those fish are easily spooked by any motion
above the water, so the cast is made as effortlessly and unobtru-
sively as possible, despite the pesky crosswind.

The big fly sails out and down into the silver-blue-green and
sinks in the current well in front of a bonefish, one that is mud-
ding, or nosing the bottom for his food. The fly will simulate his
meal and if all goes right, he'll mistake the feathered fraud for the
real thing. He does, and at once the angler raises his rod high, lets
go of the line in his line hand and the bonefish strips off fifty yards
direct from the reel quicker than it takes to read this. That's
bonefishing—that's fly fishing!

So now, let's get down to business. In order for the two scenes
and many others of infinite variety to take place, the angler must
be able to perform under all circumstances. To do this he must
have the correct balanced tackle and know how to use it.

The tools of the trade are a rod, of appropriate action, a reel
that will hold enough line and its backing, a line designed to merit
the action of the rod, a proper weight and length of leader tied to
the line and a fly to go along for the ride.

All four elements come in various sizes and kinds and it is
correct choice for the need at the moment that counts.

This is what is called "balanced tackle"; that is, tackle that in
its assembled combination delivers the fly to its destination with
an absolute minimum of effort on the part of the angler.

It is also tackle that can withstand the fight of the fish under tough conditions of fast water, high wind and snags.

It is the tackle that is the lightest and sportiest, yet not too light for proper distance casting and line handling requirements. It is designed to cast a tiny fly into a strong wind, to handle a line for the fishingest retrieve and to subdue the quarry gradually. First, some principles, and then some details.

BALANCED TACKLE

Balanced tackle means that the rod, reel, line and leader are selected for length, action, weight and capacity to best present the fly to its destination. A rod with a stiff action requires a heavier line than a soft action rod. A soft action rod with too heavy a line will not cast well. A level line will not cast as far or as easily as a double taper, and while a weight-forward "ballet" taper line does not perform well at short distances, it is required for those long casts. A leader that is too light at the butt or top end will not extend the power force in the line and present the fly properly to the water. A leader that is too heavy will not cast well nor present the fly in a straight line. A leader with a heavy butt section and a long thin section is difficult to cast, since the long thin and light section will tend to pile up. And more troubles are possible from improperly selected tackle.

Rods

Now, first of all, there are rods of bamboo—six strips or five strips or even four strips—that produce certain types of action depending upon the degree of taper from the butt section to the tip. There are also glass rods of an entirely different character of action but designed to fulfill the angler's needs. These also vary in taper and proportionately in the action. Then, rods come in certain lengths; from 6 to 9½ feet, generally. Somewhere within those lengths and tapers is the rod action designed for the type of fishing to be undertaken.

It is strongly recommended that the angler who is not too familiar with fly fishing select a glass rod or rods for his use. They are more than adequate for all fishing and will, for the most part, become as acceptable as the more subtle action of bamboo. Then, too, a bamboo rod of decent manufacture is relatively expensive and if the angler follows the usual pattern, he'll want to buy and try several types of actions over the years until he develops specific personal habits and idiosyncrasies that lead him to identify the certain types of actions he wants for his various kinds of fishing.

Lines and Leaders

There is also the proper line; double-taper, level, or weight-forward taper—sinking line, floating line, floating line with a sinking tip, and then the appropriate leader size and length for casting

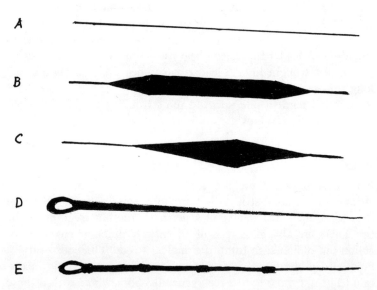

Various lines from level to double-taper to weight-forward or bullet-taper are used.

(A) Level line; (B) Weight-forward line; (C) Double-taper; (D) Single-strand factory-tapered leader; (E) Hand-tied stepped-down tapered leader.

the specific types and weights of flies to be used (see illustration). While this may sound complicated, it is stressed to impress upon the reader the importance of buying the right equipment for his needs right from the start. Wrong tackle simply will not perform right and will sooner or later lead to equipment replacements.

With the hundreds of rods made available by major rod companies and individual rod-builders, a host of variances are available. Lines, on the other hand are more standardized. Leaders —either level or tapered—are available to match all lines properly, but a great deal of freedom of choice is still available and should be exercised. Many anglers make up their own specific tapered leaders, sometimes beginning with level strands and tying them in certain lengths, thinner and thinner, until they reach the finest tippet end—needed for a specific situation. Others start with a tapered one-piece leader, adding a heavier butt section and thinner tippet end than that found on the usual store-bought leader.

The smaller the fly, the smaller the eye of the hook. The point of the leader is to make the leader, itself, as invisible to the fish as possible, therefore the lightest possible tippet section is recommended within reason and for ease of casting, with the fish's fighting strength and ability also to be considered.

All this tackle, when assembled, must be geared for the type of fishing to be done; long casts, short casts, small fish, big fish, small flies, heavy and large or wind resistant flies. The 6-foot rod that will handle a size 22 midge fly on a seven-× leader being cast a short distance in a small stream will hardly suffice for casting a big heavy and fluffy bass bug fifty or sixty feet on a wide lake, nor will it handle the bass that takes the bug. A bonefish outfit used to throw sixty feet of line and a heavy bucktail fly into a strong wind and then handle a fast running fish of six or more pounds would hardly be the set-up for fishing a narrow brushlined creek for trout merely 10 inches long.

So, the trick is to narrow the choice of equipment down fairly near the general use the tackle will get. There is no such thing as the one rod or one tackle set-up for everything. Like golf, there are several clubs for various needs on the course—from the driver on the tee to the putter on the green.

Now, to select specific tackle for specific types of fishing.

GUIDE FOR BALANCING FLY RODS WITH PROPER WEIGHT FLOATING FLY LINE

Length and Weight of Rod	Level	Double Taper	Rocket Taper	Bug Taper
7 ft. Light Action	L5F	DT5F	WF5F	——
7½ or 8 ft. Light Action	L5F	DT5F	WF5F	——
8 ft. Medium Action	L6F	DT6F	WF6F	——
8½ ft. Light Action	L6F	DT6F	WF6F	——
8½ ft. Medium Action	L7F	DT7F	WF7F	WF8F
8½ ft. Heavy Action	L9F	DT9F	WF9F	WF9F
9 ft. Light Action	L7F	DT7F	WF7F	WF8F
9 ft. Medium Action	L8F	DT8F	WF8F	WF8F
9 ft. Heavy Action	L9F	DT9F	WF9F	WF9F
9½ ft. Medium Action	L9F	DT9F	WF9F	WF9F

NOTE: Above chart is necessarily only a very general guide to probable balance between fly rod and proper line weight. For accurate balance of your particular rod, take to your dealer who will check it on a Professional Fly Line Guide Chart.

New Marking System (by the numbers)

The accepted system of marking fly line weights is based on the weight of the working part of the fly line— the front section. Exclusive of any tip on a taper, the first 30 feet of line is weighed to determine its category.

AFTMA FLY LINE STANDARDS

#	Wt.	Range	#	Wt.	Range
1	60	54-66	7	185	177-193
2	80	74-86	8	210	202-218
3	100	94-106	9	240	230-250
4	120	114-126	10	280	270-290
5	140	134-146	11	330	318-342
6	160	152-168	12	380	368-392

Weight in grains—Range allows for acceptable manufacturing tolerances.

Tackle for Average Use

Brook and stream trout fishing with occasional forays on lakes and larger bodies of water will also include fishing for panfish, shad and even bass when small flies will be used. In its extreme use, this rod, reel and line can also be used (when the angler is really experienced) for landlocked salmon, steelhead and Atlantic salmon.

The tackle will suffice excellently, for the learning period, and will still allow a wide range of fishing possibilities as noted. Once the casting, line manipulation and retrieving is mastered on this gear, the angler can then adapt his casting timing and line handling to bring out the best in tackle both lighter or heavier than the basic tackle combination at first selected.

Even for this general middle-of-the-road small game fishing tackle, there are infinite variations to fit the needs of the angler. After learning to flex a rod to discover its basic action, the angler will be able to discern the correct action for his needs and also for his personal style of fishing. Some like a very stiff or hard action. Others are more quiet and easy in their approach and would thus require a much softer or slower action rod, generally. Then, too, there is a definite reason why in a rod of, say 8 feet, there can be quite a decisive difference in actions. One may be very soft and slow throughout its length. Another might be fairly stiff in the butt section and middle with a softer tip action. The second is preferred by avid dry fly fishermen, who desire to throw a narrow bow and to whisk the dry flies in quick false casts and shoot them directly and powerfully out great distances. Others fishing basically with wet flies and nymphs with only occasional dry fly work prefer the slower action rod which will throw a wider bow and is the thing for fishing at shorter distances.

The angler who will be fishing with the bigger flies, both dry and bucktails and streamers or a brace or three weighted nymphs will prefer the longer rod with a "medium action"—not too stiff, not too limber. This rig-up will also handle dry flies as well, but not to the exacting needs of the purist and expert dry fly fisherman.

Reels

The reel must not be too heavy or too light for balance. With the reel mounted on the rod and line out through the guides, the rod should balance in the hand parallel to the ground. If the tip points up high, the reel is too heavy. If the rod points down, the reel is too light. This difference can be noted when great amounts of casting are done and long hours of fishing are scheduled. Yet, that reel must be of the correct size to accommodate the line to be used and, when the fishing will require a length of backing, it must be of a large enough diameter to house all the line needed.

The conventional reels are made in various sizes and weights by countless manufacturers hence the one to be selected is easy to find. The single-action, that is nonmultiplying, is the conventional type. It has a built-in adjustable drag so that when the angler strips line out, it doesn't overspin and cause a backlash. Actually

SINGLE-ACTION
FLY REEL

the fly reel is merely a device for carrying the line in the case of most small fish. With big fish when it is necessary to play the fish from the reel, the drag is set to a pound test well below the breaking strength of the lightest section of the leader; this assumes the latter is cushioned by the rod's springing power. Many anglers out for the extreme in fly fishing sport will use a light rod, but a reel with a large capacity for backing, which will allow the fish to run great distances since the power of the lighter rod will not be enough to stop them. This sort of specialization is mentioned here only to suggest the many possibilities an angler will enjoy once the basics are mastered.

PERSONAL NOTE

If desired, the author's selection can be used as a guide for tackle specifications. For small streams and close work, my six-foot 2-oz. rod with a light Hardy reel carrying a double-taper 4 F, 120-grain weight line I use for dry flies, midges, possibly a brace of two small nymphs. It is adequate for 20 to 40-foot casts, stretching to fifty when necessary. The little rod is bamboo, the 8-footer in this class would include the use of small bucktails and weighted nymphs.

For big streams, throwing from 40 to 65 feet of line, standard bucktails, streamers, a brace of weighted nymphs, and big Wulff-type dry flies would call for my 7½-foot glass or bamboo rod for medium length work or the 8½-footer for extended service. A 120 to 170-grain line in DT 4 F line with 25 yards of backing on a medium weight reel would suffice for medium to slow cycle casting, not fast whipping or narrow bow shooting.

For the heavy work on Montana's Gallatin, Oregon's Deschutes or for steelhead or Atlantic salmon, or on the Catskill's Esopus while after the big spring rainbows, I'd go to the 8½ or 9 ft. glass in 5½ oz. weight with a stiffer action which would allow casts up to 75 feet. While the action of the rod is fairly stiff, the casting sequence with two bucktails or weighted nymphs would still not be of the "fast" type. The line is a WF 8 F on a big reel loaded with 50 yards of backing line.

For bass bug fishing I like my 9½-foot, slow cycle rod with its WF 7 F line. Bonefish will call for the 10-footer, with a reel packed with 100 yards of backing. I attach the extension butt.

All these rods come in two or three sections. I prefer the two-section rods because of the more complete action, not stopped by too many ferrules.

FLY FISHING NEEDS AND ACCESSORIES

In addition to the flies, a subject covered later, there are specific items that will be necessary when the angler is on the stream or in a boat on a lake, or at the oceanside.

These are actually few, although there is a room full of gear on the market that is supposed to be basic equipment. Much of it, however, is actually unnecessary. The idea is to eliminate as much gear as possible and leave the energy and time for the fishing.

Boots/Waders

Boots and/or waders will make it possible to fish from a position in the water, a constant need in stream and ocean surf fishing. Boots come in hip length and extend to the crotch, held up to the belt by a snap-on length of rubber that slips on the belt. Waders allow the angler to wade deeper. They come waist-high or chest-high, the latter preferred by the pros. Those extra inches are valuable in deep wading and for protection from spray. Both types of waders and the boots are manufactured in rubber, rubberized fabric and various weights of plastic. The plastics are lighter, but the rubberized fabric "breathes" and in warm temperatures are preferred, though they are a little more expensive.

Proper fit is a must just as it is with the tux for the party—not for looks necessarily, but for free action and overall comfort.

Boots are relatively easy to fit, but waders extend above the crotch and require a close fitting to the angler's body, length of legs, and overall size. They should allow enough stretch as not to cause undue strain on the seams for it is at the seams that waders will first wear and leak.

In selecting foot size, don't guess. Plan to fish in a pair of silk socks next to the skin covered with another pair of wool (for cold) or cotton (for warm temperatures). Some anglers prefer the cotton next to their skin covered by a thick wool pair of socks for insulation against bruises. Boots should not fit tightly!

The feet or sole bottom of the boots or waders must conform to the type of stream rocks or ocean sand and weeds to be encountered. Slip-on sandals with either chain, felt or deeply scored rubber are available; the chain for the gravel and sand, the felt for slimy, or smooth bottoms and the deeply cut rubber for coarse rocks, barnacles and seaweed. The experts who fish the reefs and seaweed-covered rocks have developed actual spike bottoms for the sure grip.

The ordinary slightly cut-in rubber bottoms found on most boots will suffice under most circumstances where extreme conditions do not exist. (Wading techniques are covered later.)

Clothing

Pants are next. Here the accent is on a narrow, preferably cuffless bottom. Again proper fit and size for freedom of action is a must. Pants can be made of heavy material for cold; lighter weight for warm conditions. The bottoms are folded lightly and inserted into the socks for a smooth taper.

Upper clothes such as shirt, undershirt, etc., as the angler prefers, but for the cold, a medium-weight sweater is suggested, preferably turtleneck. Whatever is worn, remember that you want the very outer cover to be wind resistant in the form of a fishing vest, for warm weather when sleeveless sweaters and shirts are worn, or a fishing jacket is bought one size larger to fit comfortably over a heavy wool shirt and sweater combination. A wool scarf in addition to the turtleneck sweater is good when the wind begins to whip around.

The jacket should be water-repellent and contain numerous pockets for all of the spare reels, leaders, innumerable fly boxes, oils, glasses, notebooks, cameras, wallets, oranges and candy bars, compasses, cigarettes and lighters, pipes, tobacco, fly dope, a small first aid kit, fly-tying necessities, and a special rubberized compartment for the fish to be taken home.

And that's a large order so the jacket cannot be just any jacket! Special fishing jackets have been developed—some full length if you are not fishing in waders, and special short-length types for waders. (A long jacket worn over waders would get wet if the angler waded in very deep thus limiting his wading.)

The smart angler will wear a hat of some design. Hours spent in the sun or in the whipping cold take their toll on unprotected heads or heads not used to fishing exposure. A visor of sorts should be included in the design to shade the eyes and/or cover the lens of the glasses. While a hat is a personal item and individual style and preferences are strong, the hat for fishing must be selected for practical use first, and fashion only secondly.

Sunglasses

As to glasses, the poloroid lens allow seeing through the glare on the water. They are a must if the angler would not fish blindly. These can be lens designed to slip on over conventional prescription glasses, or when these are not necessary, a regulation pair of glasses preferably with larger lens. These cut out glare better, as undesirable amounts ordinarily still creep in with the usual small-size lens and frames. Paper lens cleaners should be kept handy in a high pocket that will insure their dryness—all lens tend to fog up near the water or during the damp of dawn or after dark in the evening.

Wading Staff

A wading staff, either a plain but staunch stick of wood or a cane with a sharp metal point, is needed for fast-water stretches of streams, rivers and rocky shores. The loop at its top should be attached to the belt, keeping the staff instantly available. This third leg is indispensable at times and can save the angler many occasions of hard work, pain and ducking.

Landing Net

The landing net, for the optimistic angler, is the basic must, even if the fish is going to be returned to the water. The short-handled stream net should be large enough for large fish, but it is not necessary to have a large hooped net if after fish of the smaller sizes. The stream net—either collapsible or solid frame—is attached preferably to the jacket by a short length of line, cord, leather or chain. It is worn with the net cord draped over the shoulder; the net hanging out of the way behind the action.

Boat nets have longer handles and usually larger-diameter hoops and deep bags for the big ones.

Some anglers like to combine the net and the wading staff in one piece of equipment, but this is the exception.

Personal Items

Leave the watch at home . . . learn to tell time by the sun. It is a good thing to be free of worries over time when fishing!

It is also advisable to leave the business wallet in the car or hidden in some safe place rather than carried on the person while fishing, especially wading. Even a tough climb over windfalls or a stumble into the creek might jar the wallet loose from a pocket and it might then become lost. Carry only ID card and fishing license, it's safer.

Any accessories other than those mentioned are up to the angler. As mentioned, traveling light is the object.

Finally in the list is a small knife, preferably one incorporating a sharp pair of scissors. The knife should be the small pocket variety hung by a thong inside the jacket—not a large hunting knife as usually worn in a sheath from the belt. Otherwise, how else can it be easily reached?

YOUR LOCAL TACKLE SHOP

Much good tackle at reasonable prices can be bought in the big major discount stores. Only trouble with this is that there is hardly ever anyone there with sufficient experience in actual fishing to help make the proper selection of tackle for even a well schooled angler.

It is highly recommended that beginner or expert buy his gear at a legitimate tackle store, even if he has to pay a higher price for it. This quite often is actually not the case at all since many tackle stores also offer big discounts.

The advantages of shopping at a sporting goods store are many. First of all, the buyer of the store's tackle is acutely aware of his chain store competition. He will not sell shoddy merchandise, or so-called bargain tackle since he has to stake his reputation on happy customers who will come back again and again. He also chooses tackle to suit the fishing of the region and locale, the local demands.

He also offers personalized service. He'll wind line on the reel and splice a fly line to the backing, usually at no cost. He'll also make line loops and tie special leaders. Usually he has a big selection of flies and fly rod lures and knows, because of his intimate association with his customers, which ones are catching fish.

He is local, and involved locally with his customers. Usually he is an officer of a local rod and gun or fishing club, one of the fly tying or fly casting instructors and he certainly knows how to select tackle that's balanced and can instruct the user in new or advanced techniques.

He's also a fisherman himself. He knows where to go and when and with what and he makes it his business to see to it that his customers come in to thank him for his advice and counsel.

Talking with him during the quieter hours at the store will often reveal a lifetime of fishing experiences and much lore of the area.

One of the best reasons to visit the tackle store that caters strictly to hunters and fishermen is that this is where they love to congregate to shoot the breeze. There's a feeling of brotherhood. Perhaps new friends are made on the stream and re-met in the store or vice versa. From these meetings will come new friendships and valuable interchanges of information and laughs, plus some good stories of fish that got away.

There is usually a nucleus of old timers about who have been fishing in the area for many years. From them many hints and tips can be garnered just by listening and prodding them with questions.

Anglers, home from trips to other parts of the country, will also offer lecture-like talks about their experiences and some will produce good photos of their catches to back up the ad libs.

The tackle store is a fount of catalog information. It is wise to keep up with the latest in tackle developments. These catalogs are usually available just for the asking, and while you thumb through them the questions to be answered will be directed to the store manager or even some of the customers.

Stores of this sort are humming with information about fish stocking programs, conservation projects and law changes. Many of the shops issue fishing licenses and have readily available details of the legal aspects of fishing in their state.

Clubs are formed around the informal gatherings at such stores. Many a large organization got its start from both sides of the counter.

Visit and revisit your local tackle store. You'll profit by it.

3

~~~~~~

Fly Casting Simplified

FLY CASTING IS easy. Only a few basic principles need be recognized to see how and why that small fly goes out great distances when harmony between the rod, line and leader and the angler's pressure and timing are precise.

In contrast to bait casting or spinning when a heavy lure is used and the weight of lure is a factor affecting distance and direction of the cast, the reverse is true of the tiny fly. It merely goes along for the ride. In fact, it is not necessary for the fly to be attached to the leader in order to cast a great distance with the fly rod. The fly, in fact, *retards* the leader and shortens the cast because of its weight and resistance to the wind. Fly rod casting, then, is not a job of pitching a fly out there in front and using a lot of awkward motions to do it.

The main principle of fly casting, and all rod casting for that matter, is to recognize that the rod must flex or bend to pressures in order to deliver the line and leader to its destination. For this to happen, the rod must be flexed with power driven by the hand, wrist and arm. It will bend in one direction and then in the opposite direction to the same degree. The more power exerted on it, the more bend.

It will be noticed that in the conventional cast—fore and aft, the line will have to go as far behind the angler as it will go in front of him. In order to create this force and resultant action,

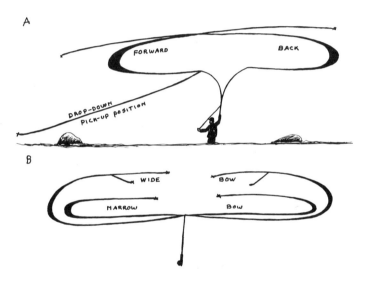

Figure 3-1. A shows the line in the air during the false cast. Note that the line goes as far backwards over the angler as it goes forward to the drop down position. The cast is actually made in two basic motions after the pick-up. One action swings the rod back and the line follows behind, straightens out behind, and then is pushed forward in the second phase which leads to the drop down.

B shows the wide bow used with wet flies and streamers. This uses a slower casting action and timing and allows a wider area during the cast so that the line will not double on itself accidentally.

B also shows the narrow bow, used in dry fly fishing, particularly the fly-drying false cast. It is also better to have the bow flat and fast for fishing into or alongside a wind.

power from the fulcrum of the action—the angler's hand, wrist and arm must be exerted upon the rod. Then things happen. [Figure 3–1 (A) (B)]

The line "picks up" this power from the rod and acts somewhat like a whip—the follow through of the action to the very end of the line.

The leader then "turns over" on the cast, lays out flat above the water and the fly lights daintily on the surface, followed by the leader and then the line. (Figure 3–2)

Figure 3-2.   Leader turns over. This is the way the line looks during the drop down. Note how the follow-through of the power imparted to the line by the rod forces the end of the leader and its fly to alight first on the water—straight and lightly to the surface.

RIGGING UP/GETTING SET TO CAST

With a set of balanced tackle—rod, reel, line and leader—on the table, the first job is to wind the backing line on the reel. In order to know just how much total line the reel will hold (both backing and tapered line), the tapered line is first lightly attached and wound onto the reel from its packaged spool or coil. Do this in an orderly way with the loop of line held vertical and wind direct to the reel so that no coiling ensues in the process. The space left on the reel between the line and the top edge of the spool shows the space left for backing line.

Now, do not attach the line to the backing, but merely wind the backing line on in the same fashion—twist-free—to the reel.

Allow a little margin, since the line will not always be wound tightly on the reel, especially its last few yards.

Now, the amount of backing required is known. Reel this line back onto the spool from which it came, cutting the section, of course. Then unwind the tapered line from the reel. Now attach the backing to the reel spool with a slip knot and make sure that a minimum of end line is present. After the backing line is reeled on, the tapered line is attached to the backing.

Next, merely roll the tapered line onto the reel. Do not put the leader on yet. The first casting steps will be done without a leader.

Some anglers who cast with their right hand, prefer that the reel be mounted with its handle to the right, the line coming out of the reel anticlockwise at the bottom or through a circular or shaped line guide plate on the "front" of the reel as it is attached to the rod.

Some prefer to have the spool handle on the left side, since with their right hand on the rod they might play the fish, using the left hand to handle line tension or take up excess slack line by cranking it back on the reel.

There is generally a keeper ring or line guide just ahead of the work handle on the rod itself. DO NOT thread the line through this, for it has another function described later. For now, thread the line up through the first guide, and leave a surplus of line hanging.

Now to assemble the rod.

One of the most important parts of the rod are the ferrules. The female ferrule is at the end of the first section or handle section of the rod. The male ferrule is at the butt end of the second section and on a three-piece rod, on the butt end of the third section or tip.

In putting the ferrules together, several cautions are in order to assure a straight and even juncture and to avoid undue strain on these delicate rod parts.

Before joining one section to another, first align all the line guides. Make sure all the ferrule sections are clean and dust or grit-free, for scratches in the soft metal will impair the rod. The guide line-up is to insure against having to later twist the sections and

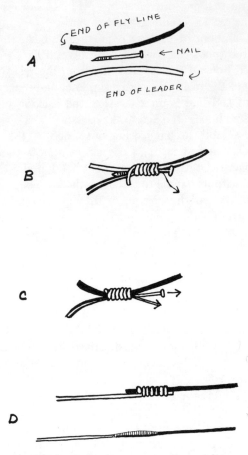

Figure 3-3. This knot is used to tie the permanent leader to the fly line and also for tying the backing line to the back end of the fly line.

Use a tapered nail or piece of small tubing. Hold the line, leader and nail alongside each other as shown in A. Allow ample overlap. Now wind the leader downward around nail and line six times and then run end of leader back along nail or through tubing under the loops as in B. Pull both ends of leader tight. Slip knot down nail, tightening by pulling both ends of leader as it goes. Slip nail out (C) and retighten by again pulling leader ends. Finally, pull line and leader tight and clip end of line and leader close to knot.

D shows the completed knot after winding with 7X thread and varnishing for a smooth covering for ease in slipping the line through the guides of the rod.

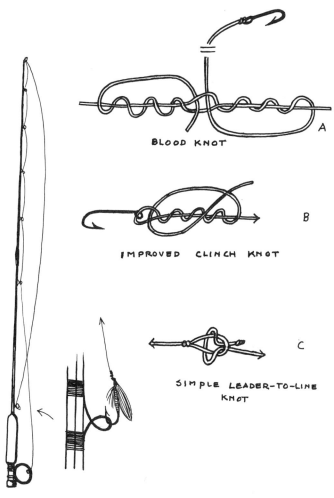

BLOOD KNOT

A

IMPROVED CLINCH KNOT

B

SIMPLE LEADER-TO-LINE KNOT

C

Figure 3-4. This is the set-up of the reel, rod, and line with the fly attached to the special ring guide, the latter used for holding the fly when it is not in use.

A is the blood knot used in tying two strands of leader together. This is for making a tapered leader and also for making an extension tippet when two or more flies are being used on the cast.

B is the improved clinch knot used for attaching the hook to the leader.

C is an alternate way of quickly attaching a leader to the fly line if it is desired to be able to change leaders quickly.

possibly thus mishape the ferrules. A little oil rubbed from the nose or hair is usually sufficient for ferrule lubricant. Do not ever put excessive oil in the female ferrule, for the original snug fit will then be spread by oil and the joint will not thereafter secure properly.

With the tip and/or second and third section of the rod together and lined up perfectly, the line is now threaded through the guides and out the end tip guide. The outfit is now ready to cast.

For learning purposes—just to get the "feel" of the outfit and perfect the use of both arms and hands—pick a practice area free from obstructions, preferably a lawn or open area free from gravel and concrete, so the line won't be damaged by undue friction and casual wear and tear.

The fore-and-aft cast and the roll cast are the two basic casts which must be mastered to fish properly. There are, of course, variations of these casts. For the purposes of this book, these are sufficient since the variations are legion. The fore-and-aft cast can be modified by the side-arm cast, the same routine, except that the cast is made parallel to the water. To change direction, the motion of the rod will become self-evident. To cast into a strong wind, a tight bow low to the water is directed. In casting across wind, allow for drift. In the upstream or downstream mend cast, a variation of the roll cast, the line is directed by the rod to the right or left during the roll and during the release, a procedure that becomes clear when actually fishing.

Many of these variant casts are described in unnecessarily elaborate detail in other books on angling, but without the ability to make the two basic casts illustrated here, the others would be quite impossible.

Fly casting is actually easy. Armed with the correct initial steps the angler soon learns to ad lib for his own needs. Remember, the main secret is to learn to wait for the line and leader to just about reach their maximum place behind the rod tip before flicking the rod forward (or backwards) again. It is in learning this little trick that most novice fly casters have their main and perhaps only difficulty.

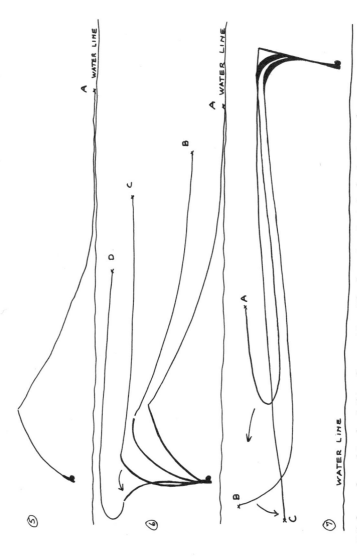

Figure 3-5 shows the rod in the drifting line position. The fly and end of the leader is on the water preparatory to the pickup. Figure 3-6 shows the action of the beginning of the pickup, A; the beginning of pressure B; C the upward and back pressure angle and D the beginning of the back part of the cast as the line is hurled through the air from the initial push on the rod. Figure 3-7 shows at A the line still coming back before it bends out; B is when the line begins to flatten out at the back of the cast. At C the line is straightened out completely. Only at this critical point does the angler begin the forward action of the cast. The pressure is spent in the rod and it has returned to the vertical position of inaction for but an instant.

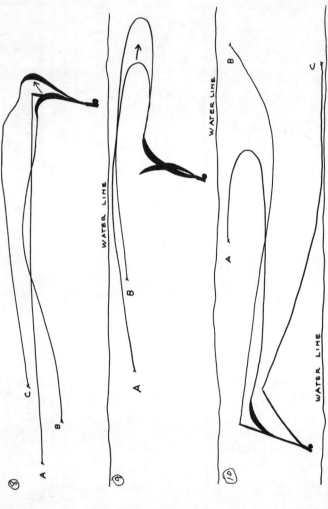

Figure 3-8 shows the line at A straightened out again, rod relaxed. B shows the beginning of the forward push of the rod and in C the line as it starts to follow along forward.

At A in Figure 3-9 is shown the midpoint of the forward throw and line bend with B showing the extent of the forward push on the rod as the line begins to follow through from the pressure.

At A in Figure 3-10 the rod is fully bent forward by the weight of the line as it unfolds. At B the line begins to drop down and at C, the rod is spent and the line follows down to the water on the drop down.

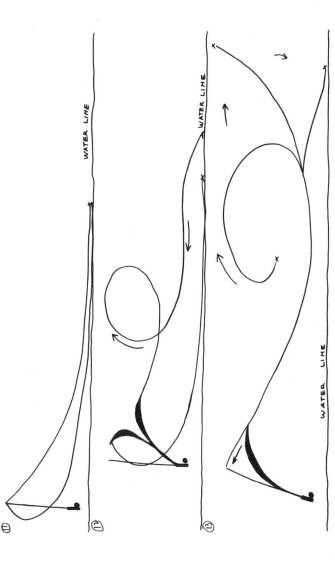

In Figure 3-11 the line is lying on the water at the beginning of the roll cast. The angler draws the line back so that it bellies out alongside him and at that instant . . .

As in Figure 3-12, there occurs the sudden, strong downward flex of the rod causing the line to raise up from the water forming a loop.

Figure 3-13 shows the result of this powerful pressure as the loop of line unfolds forward and down again to the water.

The rollcast pickup is made in the same way, but just before the line drops down as in Figure 3-12, the conventional fore-and-aft cast is begun as previously shown.

The rollcast STRIKE is made in the same manner. Instead of pulling back on strike, the conventional way it is done, a rollcast is made. This raises the line UP off the water in a quicker move to hook the fish.

SOME FLY CASTING SUBTLETIES

Only the two basic casts have been detailed in this book. There are many others that will be learned by experience. Many authors have named these casts and described them in detail, but the author feels that the angler will develop these casts himself, by learning. Many of the casts are really more difficult to describe in words and diagrams than actually experienced.

For example, in the regular fore-and-aft cast, the angler will experience certain problems. In casting the falsecast, the timing should be kept regular, but not stiffly so. A slight breeze may affect it, lowering the line too much or throwing it out of the path that was intended. This will require additional pressure on the rod, and perhaps additional line tension in order to right the situation. If a change in direction is needed the angler can, by falsecasting, gradually work his way across to another angle, or make an abrupt change in a combination of rod direction and line tension. If a stiff breeze comes up, the angler must "tighten the bow" against it. This means a more powerful action of the rod, perhaps some line tension in a modified double haul. The narrow bow and quicker back-and-forth cast will usually suffice in a stiff wind. The cast can also be made sideways to the water, or parallel to the water, a cast that is a bit more difficult to control, but needed nevertheless. When casting in under an overhanging tree, the side cast, executed in a tight bow right flat to the water is needed in order to shoot the line in under the overhang.

Mending the line is a variation of the rollcast. Suppose the angler desires to mend the line upstream for a longer drift of the fly. The roll cast is made as described, but as the pickup is begun, the rod is waved in a curve that will create a wide upstream bend in the line. As the fly comes up and out of the water, it will then light upstream of its former position. This mend can also be made without lifting the fly from the water when it is desired to merely throw an added bend of line upstream to facilitate and extend the drift of the fly.

In downstream fly fishing whether using wet flies or dry flies, the stopcast is used. The falsecast is made as usual, but when it comes time to drop the fly on the water, a certain amount of slack is necessary for a normal amount of drift. As the fly is cast forward, the rod is brought to a sudden stop. The line will then fall in slight curls, allowing the fly to drift for quite a few feet. Additional line can be rollcast out without destroying the fly's drift.

In upstream dry fly fishing, and nymphing for that matter, a right-hand or left-hand curve cast is often desired so that the leader doesn't drift straight down over the area which the fly is supposed to cover. This is simply made by turning the wrist to the right or left and *slightly* stopping the rod's action on the forward throw. This will cause the fly to swing around in the direction required, throwing a bow of leader to the side and usually above the fly. The fly then will drift right over the target without the leader drifting over the fish.

Many subtleties will be learned if the angler is a tireless experimenter. Once the basics are learned, it is then time to ad lib. That's why it is important to master the two basic casts FIRST.

4

~~~~~~

Fly Fishing Methods

PROBABLY THE MOST interesting and intriguing part of fly fishing is the tremendous amount of latitude in fly types, sizes, weights and colors which have been designed to induce fish to rise—from the palm-size bluegill/sunfish category to the mighty tarpon and tuna. Fly-tiers have spent millions of man hours (and some woman hours, too) tying concoctions which they hoped would deceive their quarry and—for the more commercially-minded—cause fishermen everywhere to rise and produce their credit cards!

The techniques involved in casting, retrieving and in generally fishing these flies are legion, though because of their design, they do call for more or less standardized uses and techniques.

Briefly, this is what it's all about.

Figure 4-1. Typical dry fly on water.

DRY FLY FISHING

Dry fly fishing for trout, bass and panfish encompasses the complete range of conditions from glassy, currentless stream pools to the wildest of fast water conditions. The streams may be slow and bending, flowing through meadows and fields, or cascading down mountain gorges. The longer streams can contain long pools, from a hundred yards to three miles or more of fast semi-broken or swift-flowing flat water that extends almost indefinitely. In the course of a mile of the average stream one can encounter shelving riffles, split riffles, steep bends, straight stretches, heads and tails of pools, backwaters and step pools. The wide shores of lakes are also blessed with infinite possibilities.

In order to fish the dry fly effectively a variety of dry fly types and styles are available. Generally, anglers like to see their flies ride high on the water and it is a necessity that the fly be dressed with stiff hackles, unsinkable bodies, and wings that cock well upright so they can be seen from a distance under tricky light conditions. For the slower water, the fly pattern can ride lower on the water so that more of the fly sits in the surface film and is thus more visible to the fish. All dry flies are touched up with fly dope to increase their bouyancy.

The dry fly imitates the dun and spinner stage of the Mayfly, the adult of the caddis, stone and crane fly, and mosquitoes and midges, the most prevalent of the aquatic insects. These flies hatch in a regular schedule during the year and can be imitated by specific patterns to be used when hatches are on, riding the surface as duns or returning to the water at twilight as spinners about to mate and then deposit their eggs. Conventional upwing, slanted wing and flat or downwing flies are usual fare as are spider flies and their variants. Two schools of thought exist; the exact imitation school and the attractor, more generalized pattern school. Take your choice. Illustrated here are basic profiles of the shapes of conventional dry flies used from coast to coast. (Figure 4–2)

Figure 4-2.   Illustrating hook eyes and profiles of typical dry flies. (1) Split-wing duck-quill winged dry fly; (2) Hairwing fly; (3) Bi-visible all-hackle fly; (4) Downwing dry fly; (5) Spider fly; (6) Deep-riding soft-hackle dry fly; (7) Woolyworm, Palmer-type dry fly, low-riding; (8) Midge pupa dry fly.

Some tiers have decided that wings are not necessary on dry flies and have designed their patterns accordingly. Others have decided that wings are necessary and that hackle is not. Most conventional flies are tied with both, however. Hook sizes range from 22 small to 8 large for most trout fishing, while 10's approach the small Wulff-type hair-wing large flies and bass bugs in size and usage. Lightweight hooks with turn-down eyes are the most common, though in the smaller patterns, up-turn eyes are preferred since the strike of the hook is UP rather than down. The spider flies are usually tied best on turn-up eyes.

Dry fly fishing stems from English tradition; it is upstream casting, basically; though across-stream casting with a short drift, direct downstream casting on a slack line is often used. In broken water, the roll is often employed to present the fly to the water in quick cast succession to cause fish to rise.

Unless there is a specific rise (when the trout are breaking the

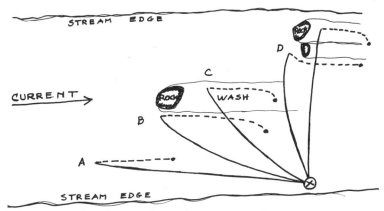

Figure 4-3. This diagram shows the conventional dry fly approach to general stream angling.

The dry fly is generally cast directly upstream and allowed to drift straight down toward the angler as in A. This direction is altered as shown at B with a slight across-stream delivery of the fly to the upper side of the midstream rock. The fly is allowed to drift down the side wash of the rock and then retrieved. The cast C, to the center of the wash must be quickly followed by raising the rod tip in order to have the fly float naturally. The fast water run beside the rock will tend to grab the line before the fly has drifted very far.

The direct across-stream cast toward the rocks is also standard procedure in dry fly fishing, but again the rod must be held high and slack held to a minimum. Direct downstream casting (not shown here) is also done by stopping the fly before it alights on the water in order to back up some slack for the downstream drift. Line can be fed out to the fly as needed until time for the pickup.

surface, feeding on the insects) the duns are floating on the current or the spinners are dipping into the water to deposit their eggs—there is little sign of actual surface feeding. The best system then, is to fish/hunt, that is, to cast over likely feed lanes, runs, eddies, and even into the center of glassy still water in order to provoke a strike from the fish, allowing the fly to drift naturally as long as possible. The heads of pools, just below the white water or the tail of the pool as it shapes off into runs are likely places for long casts and long drifts.

Except in backwaters, still waters or soft glides, line and leader drag (surface commotion due to the leader frightening the trout when the fly is whisked away unnaturally) is not a big problem to the dry fly fisherman working our generally moving waters. In fact, drag can be an advantage at times since such surface commotion does seem to attract fish to rise to the moving fly, even though the action is unnatural. Many anglers actually create surface disturbance by bouncing or dragging their flies across the ripples in short jerks.

Midge fishing using size 20 or 22 dry flies is done generally upstream with as little drag as possible. The flies require the lightest leader tippet.

Nor is dry fly fishing limited to the time of the rise. Many dry fly fishermen are content to try to bring up or raise a trout rather than to search them out with wet flies or nymphs, even though the fish might be seen actively feeding below the surface on rising nymphs.

As stated elsewhere, dry fly fishing demands the casting of a fairly tight bow for drying the fly and a more accurate delivery of the fly with a minimum of slack to the water.

As a specific pattern selection, see chapter 8, The Fun of Fly Tying for selected flies and their dressings.

Figure 4-4.   Wet fly in water.

WET FLY FISHING

Wet fly fishing is divided into three categories; the standard small wet flies of conventional design, the nymph and the steelhead fly. All are fished below the surface, that is, they are rarely doped to float although they are fished much of the time in the surface film.

Standard British wet flies and their variants, American patterns developed to imitate specific insects in various stages of the hatching season have become classics and duplicate the American dry fly patterns listed in the fly tying chapter. These smaller flies are fished one, two or three to a leader, tied on tippets which extend from the basic leader (from the end of the joining barrel knot) (see diagram).

Nymphs have been developed during the past forty years to also imitate the nymphal and larval phase of the aquatic insects. These are sometimes weighted under the dressing or fished on a weighted leader (diagram). Since the active rise follows the drift of the insects toward the surface, the fish feed for a longer time beneath the surface and thus nymphs are most effective.

Figure 4-5. Nymphs.

The standard steelhead fly is a more generalized form of wet fly that imitates either insects or small minnows or trout fry. Very few of the patterns are attempts to imitate any specific food. Some of these patterns are quite bright and their dressings somewhat complicated, approaching the simpler British Atlantic salmon flies.

Down-and-across-stream wet fly technique is standard under all conditions of water from the largest and fastest streams to the little meadow creeks. The object of such wet fly fishing is to search out trout that are either actively feeding on underwater insects

drifting toward the hatch or drowned aquatic insects drifting in the
surface film. Land-bred insects also make up a large part of fish
diet and so fall into the category of dead drifting insects, as they
swirl in the current.

One of the most effective techniques, especially after a rain, or
in the early morning and late evening, is to fish these flies on the
surface along the runs and eddies, dappling the flies and actually
dragging them across the smooth water. The surface disturbance
must imitate the struggling form of the insect either hatching or
returning to the water to lay its eggs. In this instance the fly is
fished almost in the manner of the active dry fly.

The steelhead fly, on the other hand, is fished wet, near but not
necessarily on the surface, yet generally down much deeper in the
bigger waters. It is not generally fished in the active style of the
bucktail or streamer imitating an active minnow, but drifted in a
combination of swimming and drifting with the current. The steelhead, ascending the river to spawn in the manner of the Atlantic
salmon is not necessarily actively feeding on insects. He's looking
for salmon eggs drifting down from above, so the big steelhead fly
is considered a reminder of the type of minnow or large insect
upon which he was feeding before he ventured out into the ocean.

Figure 4-6.   Samples of steelhead flies.

Listed in the fly tying chapter are patterns in all three categories; standard wet flies, nymphs and steelhead flies.

Actually, most of the standard British wet flies of small size are basic on American waters as are some of the generalized nymph patterns. Only the steelhead flies are a distinct addition to the family of patterns. During the past twenty years, with the advent of over a million fly tiers in the United States, literally thousands of small wet fly and nymph patterns have been invented. Of these, a small percentage have been given broad use and their success has become known. It will be many years before the nymph, particularly, will have become standardized, if it ever does, in the manner of conventional wet flies (see chapter 8).

Nymph fishing has become a science as imposing as that of the dry fly purist category. As a method it is considered to be much more scientific and scholarly in its exact imitation attempts than the purist school of dry fly fishing. However, there is no "class" distinction between the two schools as to which is the more sporting art form.

Fifty years ago in the United States, there was no such thing as nymph fishing. It was either wet fly or dry fly or a general combination of both. Standard wet fly patterns were either imported from England or tied to basic English patterns. These were largely fished in the "chuck and chance it" tradition, usually dappled on the surface, allowed to swim in the current. A few anglers weighted their leaders or tied weighted flies, especially for early season fishing when the water was high and discolored or at times when there were no hatches in evidence.

Streamer and bucktail flies were developed to imitate stream minnows which furthered the art of wet fly fishing, since many of these patterns were small and could be suggestive of the larger stream insects such as the stone fly and dobsonfly larvae. Today,

Figure 4-7. Some streamer flies.

"wet fly" can mean anything from a legitimate Mayfly nymph imitation to a tiny minnow.

Since the advent of nymph fishing which got its start as suggested by such artists as Ray Bergman, Edward Hewitt, Larry Koller, James Leisenring and this author, through books and magazine articles, the tying of wet flies as nymphs and strict nymph patterns have almost changed the "wet fly" system. Add to this the "flymph," as tied and promoted by Vernon Hidy—a combination nymph and wet fly to be used at insect emergence time —and it is plain there is quite a conglomerate of what can still be called a wet fly.

Tackle development in the form of fast action-distance casting rods has also had its effect on wet fly fishing. Most American anglers have fallen for the attractions of distance casting. One rarely finds an angler fishing with a short line, particularly on large streams and rivers. The wet fly is difficult to control at a long

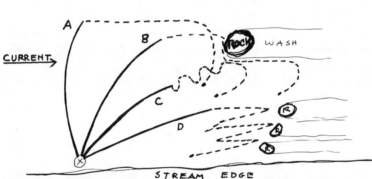

Figure 4-8.   Four standard ways to fish the wet fly.

One is A, in the across-stream cast, allowing the fly to sink in the current as it descends. Line tension at the end of the drift pulls the flies around in an arc at just the point of expected action in front of a rock or snag, for example.

B is a more downstream approach with the extended drift in order.

C is the cast allowing much slack line so that the fly will drift as directed and then be retrieved a bit upstream.

D is the direct downstream cast where the fly is allowed to drift and is retrieved on the surface or near the surface, allowed to sink down and drift down again as many times as is practicable for the cast.

distance so many anglers either fish with small streamers and bucktails or exact nymphal imitations.

The school of exact imitation in nymphal patterns has all but eliminated the pretty flies of yesteryear. In their stead are the more drab and subtle insect colors in most artificials, both wet fly and nymph. Almost every famous stream has one or more fly tiers in residence and they do a land-office business in patterns that produce on their stream and those in the immediate area. Some of these patterns are designed for specific insect hatches or minnow species.

In fact, the technical difference between dry fly and wet fly fishing is sometimes hard to define. Many dry fly anglers do not dope their floating flies, but fish them "in the film" of the water surface, and others using, say, the wooly worm pattern, a fly that can either sink or float, sometimes dope the wet fly version to float. The conventional wet fly fished on the surface, dappled or dragged across the top of the water might also be termed dry fly fishing.

So, in this era of much change and development by so many fly tiers and anglers bent on experimentation, the legitimate and dogmatic purisms of the past are all but disappeared from the angling scene. This reflects the spirit of Americans—that of discarding the conventional if results of better quality can be gained by unorthodox experimentation and daring.

STREAMERS AND BUCKTAILS

The basic principle of and reason for the streamer fly and its variant, the bucktail, is to present to the fish a form of bait fish upon which the game fish feeds. It is a long fly in comparison to the conventional short shank wet fly, though some streamers and bucktails are sometimes tied on conventional long shank heavy wet fly hooks. The fly presents a slim silhouette in the water, the short, sparse underhackle generally slanted back toward the bend of the hook. In some ways it is similar to the traditional large wet fly used in Atlantic salmon fishing; in fact, many of the more complicated patterns rival the salmon patterns in complexity and beauty. It requires a heavier leader than used with smaller wet and dry flies.

The formalized streamer fly is tied on a heavy diameter long shank hook with turn-down eye. Some patterns call for tails, most have wool or chenille bodies, some laced with gold or silver ribbing. The basic streamer part of the fly is made with two hackle points turned inward toward each other to form a stiff center. Then a cheek is added topped with jungle cock. Short soft hackle is added to the throat (see fly tying chapter).

Figure 4-9.   Streamer fly in water.

The formalized bucktail is tied on a similar hook with similar body, but the streamer part is made from animal hair such as deer and Polar bear or any long hair including that from the back of a

Figure 4-10.   Typical bucktail streamer fly.

dog! Sometimes the clumps of hair are tied in series to present a wider, long spread. This fly is generally cheeked only with jungle cock, though a cheek feather can be added. The throat hackle is optional.

The bucktail-streamer is tied with the bucktail tied in first and two long hackle feathers then tied in on either side with the usual dressing. The streamer bucktail is just the reverse, with the hackle points tied in first and the bucktail added in later.

The illustrations show the proportions of the dressings and the variants.

These flies can be weighted by wrapping flat lead around the shank of the hook before the body is wrapped. They can also be weighted as shown (see fly tying chapter) by the addition of split BB shot or strips of wrap-around lead to the leader.

The fishing technique falls into basic categories. The most common and fruitful method is to cast the streamer across stream, letting it bend down in the current, sinking a bit on the drift and then retrieved in a jerking motion in a semi-circle until it is picked up for the recast. Good spots are casts made upstream from a central rock or snag, along an overhanging bank or alongside a sandbar or line of rocks.

The direct downstream cast is made by stopping the line in the air before the entire length of cast is out, thereby allowing slack line to fall. This gives the fly time to sink deeper. The fly is then retrieved in short jerks back upstream in combination with an across-stream pattern until the retrieve is concluded.

Up-and-across-stream streamer fly fishing is accomplished by casting the fly on a steep angle upstream, allowing it to drift a bit to sink and then retrieving it in jerks when the fly is about squared to the opposite bank of the stream. The direct upstream cast to a rock, current eddy, or snag is made in the manner of the dry fly. The lure is allowed to sink and then is retrieved a bit faster than it would ordinarily drift in the current until time for pick-up.

One particularly attractive method especially in fast and white water is to cast the fly into the most active water, then retrieve the fly on the surface creating as much of a fuss as possible by rod manipulation. The fly is literally skipped upon the water surface and raced toward the rod.

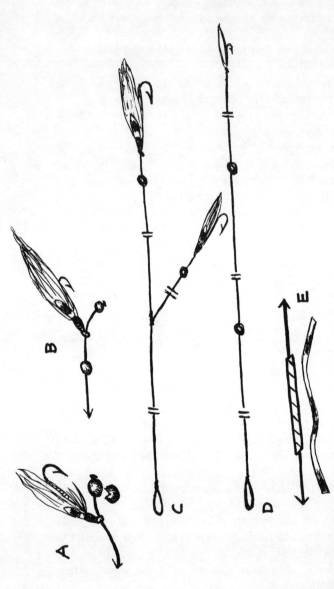

Figure 4-11. Various ways to weight the leader to sink flies in the current.
(A) The split shot lead is clamped on AFTER the fly is threaded on the end of the leader. The end of the leader is knotted so the weight will not slip off.
(B) Two weights, one before the fly, the other after it.
(C) Split-shot clamped on the leader in two places, one on the extension tippet and the second one just before the fly.
(D) Two weights evenly distributed on the leader for ease in casting.
(E) Wrap-around strip of lead is mounted around the leader as an alternate method.

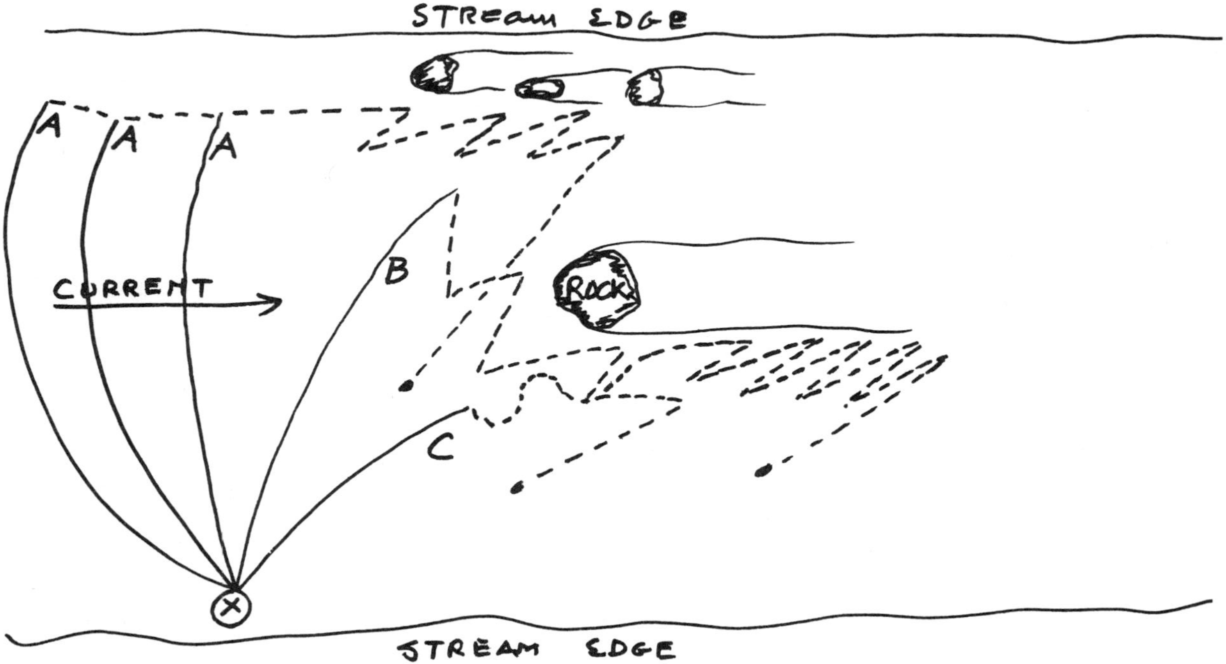

Figure 4-12. The bucktail and streamer imitate stream minnows upon which trout feed. Standard casts include the direct across-stream cast made for a drift and alternate upstream short-jerk retrieve. This cast can also be made farther upstream for a longer drift depending on conditions. If it is desired to sink the fly during the drift, the furthest upstream angle is suggested.

B affords a down-and-across-stream angle for back and forth erratic jerking fly retrieval, with a long series of retrieves before the pickup.

C is the wet-fly-like delivery of the fly on slack line, to be absorbed during the drift.

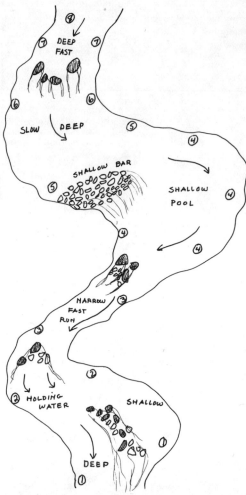

Figure 4-13. This is a typical "bendy" trout stream showing all possibilities of conditions, holding water, fast runs, shallow bars and pools. Note that the positions for casting are ALL along the EDGE of the stream, not in the actual water at all. Actually, if the stream is not too broad, most if not all of the fishing could be done from ankle-deep spots along the edge, thereby leaving the water untouched and the fish undisturbed. Study these casting positions and see how all types of flies could be cast—up, across, across-and-down and directly downstream for retrieve back to the angler.

In contrast, the most productive technique in slow water or pools is to allow the fly to sink deep to the bottom and then in short jerks the fly is retrieved slowly across the bottom.

Combinations of all these techniques can be used in even a short stretch of stream depending on bottom contours, variation of currents, etc.

On the wide and fast large streams and rivers, it is advisable to cast with a long rod of eight-and-a-half or nine feet, fairly stiff action and weight-forward tapered line. This tackle allows for short-line spot casting to specific targets with planned retrieves in mind. It also allows reaching out over the stream, above the fast water of midstream in order to cast and fish the fly through the pockets.

Big slow pools and lakes are also likely places to use the bucktail or streamer for bass, trout and other gamefish such as pike and musky. Trolling is the other form of streamer use, and in the case of northern landlocked salmon, lake trout or the three stream trout species, tandem-hooked streamers are commonly used. These generally imitate the longer and larger cisco herring or smelt upon which these fish feed. These are tied, as shown, with two hooks joined together with a single piece of nylon. They are trolled about a hundred feet behind the boat or canoe, or in the case of a big pool, cast as far as possible, allowed to drift down in the current and then retrieved back upstream.

The shorter conventional bucktails and streamers are tied to imitate the prevalent stream minnows such as the black-nosed dace, stream shiner, shad minnows and a host of other minnows that inhabit specific waters.

In contrast to some forms of wet fly fishing, the streamer is always fished in an active manner rather than simply drifted in the current.

Though third in popularity to small wet and dry fly fishing, the streamer and bucktail is a favored method if the angler is after big fish especially when there is no insect feeding or surface hatch activity in evidence. They are most effective in the early spring when the water is high and slightly discolored.

For bass and trout the Black Ghost, Green Ghost, and Gray

Ghost are favorite lake-stream patterns in streamers and the Light
Edson Tiger, Dark Edson Tiger, Squirrel Tail, Black-nosed Dace
and Micky Finn are popular. American fly tiers are specialists in
invention of this fly form and thousands of patterns are available
for their local waters.

BASS BUGS

The basic principle of and reason for the bass bug, is to present a
floating lure on the fly rod that either imitates bugs, moths, mice,
or some form of struggling form of life to the bass. Even the
largest dry flies are not large or heavy enough to cast long distances and do not remain on the surface once popped. Only the fly
rod is used with the bass bug, the latter being too light to cast with
any practibility with the conventional spinning rod or bait casting
rod.

Figure 4-14.   Typical bass bugs.

In order to create a "bug" of this sort medium-length hooks of
sizes 10 to 4 are used. The main body of the bug can be fashioned
much the same as the larger wood or plastic floating-popping
plugs used in spinning and bait casting. To this body is attached
tail feathers or fur, and fur wings. Some patterns even call for
allround hackle both in front and on the back of the bug body.
Many bugs are tied on a basic cork body. Some experts have also
devised a method of tying in bunches of deer hair which is then
clipped to the shape desired for the body, leaving the long ex-

tended hair for the tail and wings as an alternate to feather tails and wings. Some use both! In some cases, if the bug is not too heavy and wind resistant, a spinner is attached ahead of the lure or a spinner blade is attached to the bend of the hook.

Also in the class of the bass bug is the popping plug without any fur or feathers attached to it. This resembles the conventional spinning-bait casting plug but is made small enough to cast with the bass bug fly rod.

The main problem in designing these lures is to find a balance between the attractiveness of the lure when retrieved in a popping routine and its wind resistance and casting qualities. A bug that is too heavy is difficult to cast as is one that is too light and too wind resistant. A compromise is arrived at in almost every style of bug that is popluar.

Quite naturally the bass bug fisherman selects his lures to cast as far as possible with the tackle at hand. Special taper rods, lines and leaders are devised to help him do so.

As to the rod, this must be stacked with utmost power. The conventional heavy and long wet-fly rod is not enough nor is the conventional Atlantic salmon taper.

While these will cast bugs a short distance, they are not powerful enough for the distance casts often demanded. A special "bug taper" is required that calls for a stiff butt section, strong middle and slow, tapered tip section so that the heavy weight-forward tapered line can be manipulated on the retrieve and cast so that the line and lure will remain high off the water, often into or at an angle to a strong wind. The weight of the bug demands also that the tip of the rod be strong enough to "turn over" the lure so that it lands directly straight out to an accurate target. Since bass bugging is sometimes done in lily pads and grass, not to mention shoreside snags and rocks, casting accuracy is a must.

Casting is done either from a small boat or canoe to the shoreline or some mid-lake grass flat or gravel roof. Most effective bug fishing is done before and during the night and just at dawn, when the lake is quiet and big fish are on the feed.

The actual fishing technique with the bug is to cast it to the target, let it rest there for a few seconds (unless a big bass has

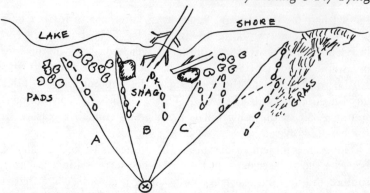

Figure 4-15. Bass bugging is generally done along the shoreline near and around lily pads, snags and grass—the lairs of big bass. From a position off shore within comfortable casting distance—from fifty to sixty feet—either wading or from a boat, the angler can poke his bug in between the pad clusters and pop, rest and pop the bug as shown.

It is sometimes advisable to roll-cast the bug after popping to a slightly different position without retrieving the bug for a recast. This is down as shown in B and C. The long retrieve of a bug cast just to the edge of the grass is another good bet.

struck it) then pop it, gently at first, retrieving it a few inches to pop it again. This routine is followed as the bug is gradually retrieved to within easy pick-up distance whereupon the bug is recast to the same spot or to another shoreside target.

The strike is almost always harsh, quick and powerful. Often the bass will be lured from deep water into the snag or grass shallows all at once or by degrees as the bug is popped. Once hooked, the bass heads for the snags on the bottom or to the side and the powerful rod must literally lift him out into the open water for the battle.

Tackle balance is most important. The rod, line and leader are selected for the general type of bug-weight-air-resistance equation. When a smaller or larger bug is used, the leader is usually changed to fit.

This casting requires the use of the single-haul or double-haul, and line that will shoot a long distance. "Double-haul," or "double line haul," incidentally, refers to the techniques by which the caster controls line with his free hand. Assume, for instance, a right-handed caster, working the rod, casting with his right hand; his left hand will endeavor to keep the line taut at all times. It will also strip extra line off the reel at times to add to the line in the air. But with this left hand control of the line the angler can also add extra pull, power and acceleration to the cast. In distance casting the idea is to bring the rod up to full load with essentially only five motions: pick-up, lay back, speed back, speed forward then shoot. If in the "speed back" phase, the angler senses a lack of sufficient speed and rod flex, he uses his line hand, pulling on the line in a single or double-haul, to keep the line traveling at full speed to prevent it from dropping—its natural tendency near the end of the "lay back" and "speed forward" stages. Properly done, the "double-haul" technique adds substantially to casting distance.

Bass bug fishing has been popular in America for about fifty years and the patterns for these bugs have never become standardized. Many of the basic ones have not even gained popular names. They are, it seems, tied instead to certain styles as specific demands dictate.

FLY FISHING FOR RIVER BASS

To the fly fisherman river smallmouths are closely akin to big trout in many of our better trout waters. In some cases, the lower reaches of the best trout streams in the East contain large populations of both small and largemouth bass. Fortunately for the angler many rivers that cannot any longer (or never did) support a trout population have excellent bass fly fishing available. While the rivers may be slower with less white water, rushing rapids and the like, there are, nonetheless, pools, riffles and deep long slicks where the bass like to feed and reside.

When river bass fishing is considered by the average bass fisherman lures and bugs are thought of at first. But when the trout-oriented angler goes after them he is more prone to use the same general flies used in regular trout fishing. Both schools of thought have their merits on a bass river.

The trout fisherman can arm himself with large and fluffy dry flies almost as large and bugs as small as the smallest fly rod bugs and even some of the ultra-light spinning flies. One of the best bass lures is a combination of the spinner and the fly. One of the best trout flies that can be used in river dry-fly fishing for bass is the cork-bodied or hairbodied dry fly, which is nothing more than a reduced size bass bug.

Bass are more active during the summer months in comparison with trout found in the same water. Where trout are not found at all the bass are comfortable and not loggy. Selective, perhaps, although not to nearly the same degree.

The first introduction to fly fishing for bass might come as the trout angler is working the lower stretches of his favorite trout stream where a lake below supplies the bass that migrate up the river for cooler water during the summer months. He'll be dry fly fishing at the head of a pool when the mighty splash he thinks is being caused by a whopper brown trout is in reality a bass of much smaller size.

Pound for pound, a horsey smallmouth will offer twice the fight of an equal weight brown trout, particularly in the summer months of warmer water. At this time of the year, the browns feed less, become slim and snakelike, and are not nearly as fighty as they were in May.

The summer bass, then, is the fish for the hot months.

All the techniques and strategies of good trout fly fishing can and should be employed. The accent can be on bucktails and underwater flies in the deeper sections of the stream, but do not neglect the buggy floating flies that can be skittered across the surface of pools and stiller waters.

The confirmed bass angler, accustomed to using his bass tackle, has a new thrill in store for him when he ventures forth after bass with trout gear. For that matter, it will lead him to fly fishing for trout as well.

Tackle requirements are the same, though for most of the heavier bass bugs, a longer rod, heavier line and staunch leaders are required.

Most bass rivers where trout are not found offer much in the way of trolling. Long feathered streamers and big and gaudy wet flies can be trolled or cast from the boat to the shoreline and especially into the pocket water at the bends of streams and in the backwaters (see chapter 7, Fishing Lakes and Artificial Impoundments).

SALTWATER FLY FISHING

Saltwater fly fishing owes nothing to European tradition. True, some anglers on the other side of the pond have probably fished for saltwater fish with the fly rod, but it was in America that the real start of this sport specialty is credited. Many of us, some forty years ago, took fly rods to the surf, bays, inlets and open ocean to "do it the hard way" with the fly rod. When I was 10 years old, I borrowed my father's twelve-foot salmon rod, big reel and silk line and caught Quoddy pollock with it. Those fish took white bits of a handkerchief on a cod hook like there was no tomorrow. Striped bass were my next try and Long Island Sounders got quite a shock seeing stripers landed with a fly rod. Then came sailfish, tarpon and snook.

Then a few anglers, fishing in more southern waters, began to popularize the bonefish as the epitome of fly rod sport. From there on in, all species were fair game including sailfish and marlin! On the West Coast, bonita and other deepwater fish including the barracuda were taken on fly rods and the sport was born. Bluefish, mackerel, weakfish and sea trout, pollock, snook, tarpon, bonefish, lady fish, sail fish, pompano, permit and any fish that could be cast to in shallow water became fair game. Some even troll using the charter boat outrigger and then fighting the fish with the fly rod when the big one strikes.

But for some time there was one big problem. Freshwater tackle was simply not designed for use in salt water. Ferrules and reel seats corroded. Rod finish broke down quickly. Lines crumbled. Special leaders with steel wire had to be invented in sizes that could be cast properly. Bamboo rods wore out too quickly.

With the advent of glass rods, the new plastic lines, bigger and stronger reels with noncorrosive qualities were built and began to be mass-produced. The sport was now on its way. It remained for a few experimenters in touch with the tackle companies to develop better functioning equipment for an eager new market signifying an entirely new phase in sport fishing.

As to the flies used, the choice has become quite simple and nowhere near as complicated as with trout or bass flies. Saltwater flies are tied to imitate the color and action of bait fish, be they herring pilcher, squid, shrimp, speering or worms on the East Coast, or herring, small baitfish and anchovies on the West Coast.

Figure 4-16.   Sample saltwater fly.

All that is needed is to balance the casting outfit to the flies to be used and the task at hand.

Tackle needs vary, but the most important qualification of any tackle is that it be able to cast a heavy fly well, far and with some degree of accuracy; cast it into a wind; handle it in fast current or tide rip; and pick it up off the water efficiently for a recast. The reel must be large enough to hold a weight-forward tapered line of the heaviest design, and also include at least 100 yards of nylon backing. Leaders can be tapered, but they are not necessarily long. In fact, short leaders of thin diameter stainless steel are required when trying for fish noted for their teeth or sharp and hard mouths. The nylon simply will not stand the wear and tear with all but the exceptionally few smaller species.

While tackle has not become too standardized, a general requirement would include a glass fly rod, two or three section, of at least 9 and preferably 10 feet in length with a wide swinging action, not too stiff a butt section, and not too stiff a tip. The action of the saltwater cast is not fast and whippy as it is in most freshwater work. Remembering that the saltwater fly is much heavier than the usual freshwater bucktail or streamer, the cast motion will have to be longer and slower, the backcast kept high, the double-haul a necessary method of adding power to the cast. The sinking line is most often used.

Since most of the fishing will require fighting the fish from the reel, the angler must learn NOT to play the fish from the line handling the line ONLY when retrieving slack in order to control the fish. When the fish makes a run, this line in the hand is dropped, otherwise the line can cut the fingers in an instant. When the fish does run, the usual pose is to hold the rod with both hands high above the head so as to keep as much line off the water as possible and the line free from underwater snags and barnacled rocks, especially when the fish is being fought in the shallows.

Actual fighting technique has to take into consideration the limited amount of line that can be carried on the reel. The rod is brought into play to much greater extent than with conventional saltwater tackle. The fish must be killed as quickly as possible and the long powerful fly rod makes up for the difference. The angler must use power from the instant of the strike until he has his fish, otherwise it can run away with him. There is no thrill like fighting a big fish on saltwater fly fishing gear, as thousands of addicts will attest. (Refer to list of saltwater fish species and to favored flies in chapter 8.)

Perhaps the biggest natural difference encountered in ocean fishing that does not exist when fishing in lakes or most rivers is the tide. Every six hours the ocean's water "rises" and every six hours it "falls". This action keeps life in the ocean moving in a predictable routine. Learn the schedule of events in this and plan strategies accordingly. As the tide comes in, it brings baitfish into the shore and inlets, and when it "ebbs", the baitfish drop down again. The big fish know this and wait for them. The tide has its definite effect on the habits of fish. They are more lively as the tide is coming in. The fly fisherman imitating the baitfish merely tries to imitate the real thing in its natural cycles. The gamefish will surely be close by.

WADING TECHNIQUE AND SAFETY

Walking, scrambling along the rocky shores, over windfalls and into the muck, gravel and rocks of the stream, lake or seaside is one thing most people are capable of doing without much thought.

Wading in unfamiliar boots or in bulky, restricting waders is something else. For one thing, the angler is dealing with water, still or with a current, trying to find his way over a bottom he cannot see too well, sometimes not at all. A "feel" has to be developed—a kind of seeing with the feet; feeling along slowly and carefully. When a stream bottom is swept by a fast current, rocks and gravel including stones that will give way, turn over and upset one's balance, it behooves the angler to learn quickly to take small and short steps, to slide instead of step, and never to place his weight on the forward foot until solid ground or bottom has been identified. Add a bit of slime and moss to the rocks and the prospects of slipping and falling are greatly increased. This is true in wading a stream, a lake or the rocky shore of an ocean reef, beach or inlet.

Some people have a very good sense of balance. If an angler is so blessed, all well and good. Others have to develop it. The best advice is proceed with caution, looking ahead to try to spot deep holes, sharp rocks and snags, or soggy and muddy areas that might mire the feet. In stream wading, it is always wise to first try to plot the wading course by studying the water. Try and wade where the currents are broken by large boulders and shallower areas. Wading in these slacks takes a lot less energy. When wading downstream and out into the river on an angle, make sure that several good optional return courses are available to avoid having to wade back upstream against the current to reach the shore and shallows. And don't get stuck out on a peninsula with no good return route!

Armed with the best foot gear possible (see accessories) the angler will be equipped to cope with the worst conditions. It is merely a matter of learning, sometimes the hard way, to take it easy, plotting a safe course ahead of time. In fast, tricky water use the wading staff.

In deep water wading such as is done in and along big pools and open stretches of salmon and trout streams, the angler will probably be wading hip deep and sometimes even close to the top of the waders. If he steps into a hole, he's in over the top of his waders. When in doubt, slip one foot ahead of the other slowly without taking the weight off the base foot.

Actually, when wading a trout stream it is imperative that the angler wade quietly and slowly. Often fish will be seen feeding on or near the surface right alongside or ahead under the rod tip. Quite often after standing in one position for awhile, the angler will notice trout gathering behind him in the slack water!

Most anglers wade where they should fish and fish where they should be wading, therby missing a lot of good action. Learn to read the water, stay in the protected shallows and fish the runs, riffles and slacks (see figure 4-17).

READING THE WATER

Note the current lines and what is causing them, remembering that the fish do not lie in the fast water but often right beside it in a slack water slick, hole or behind an obstruction, rock or ledge of rocks. That's where the fish are. It is better to wade a little distance away, standing aside from that area and casting to it. The smart wader seldom has to enter the stream any deeper than up to his knees, since good tackle and casting ability allows him to place his flies in the potent parts of the stream or tide rip.

Shown here are samples on where to wade and how to cast and fish various waters.

Figure 4-17. This is an aerial sketch of a typical pool on a medium-sized trout stream. Assuming that the angler wants to start fishing upstream he would start at (1) and work his way up. Note that the pool contains broken rapids at the tail with an undercut bank to the right and a vast shallow water area to the left almost extending to the top of the pool. The deep run in the center is the hot spot with the broken rapids and boulder "holds" at the top of the pool. Fished properly, such a pool can produce much action. Fishing time could involve a whole day of slow wading and careful casting. First fish it upstream with dry flies or small wets or nymphs, then reverse and fish it downstream with bucktails and weighted nymphs.

Starting at No. 1, cast up and across to the tail of the rapids allowing the flies to drift out the cast. Work up to (2) and cast directly to the sides of the rocks. At (3) work both upstream and across and down through the rocks. On the right, (4) and (5) can work the undercut bank or from the left shallow position, the top of the rocks and the center current. (6) is a good position for deep and long casts up toward the head of the pool. (7) is perfect for casts right to the lip of the pool working around the rocks.

Fishing the pool downstream from (8), the bucktails can be slithered between and among those rocks and (7), (6) and (5) are good spots from which to cast into the deep water. (4) and (3) are perfect locations for spotcasting bucktails, streamers and weighted nymphs to the rocks for long drifts in the rapids.

Note that at no time has the angler entered into the good water nor taken a position that might scare the fish. If the angler were to wade right through the center runs, the fish would be disturbed along the entire pool and it would probably be considered as being "fished out."

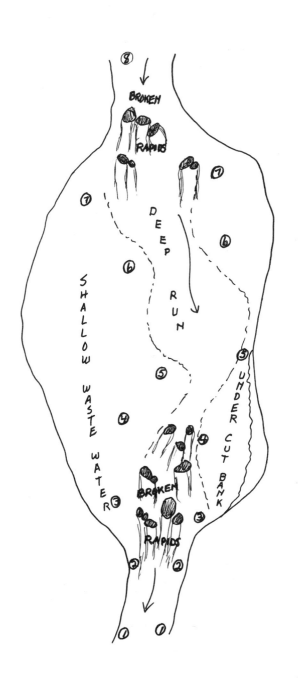

5

~~~~~~

Striking, Playing
and Landing

ONE OF THE basic reasons why fly fishing for both fresh and saltwater game fish is much more active, thrilling and fun, is because of the characteristics of the fly rod itself. Being longer, it allows much more flex than the shorter spinning, bait casting and conventional surf rods. Not that the fly rod is any less effective than the others. Actually it is more so!

But, in order to bring into play the force of this kind of a rod, the angler must synchronize his rod arm-hand, line arm-hand and, in fact, put his whole body into the act. The fly reel, being limited as to line content, must be taken into consideration; fly fishing demands that the rod make up the difference in killing power so that the fish does not run as far and as long as with the shorter rods of other techniques. The battle that follows then is strenuous!

CORRECT ROD AND LINE HANDLING

Given a rod with enough backbone in the tip to set the hook once the fish hits and the angler pulls back sharply, the hook must sink deep in mouths of fish that are sometimes very hard, bony and tough. Once hooked, the playing must be tight and on a taut line. In the case of extremely soft-mouthed fish, light terminal leaders and small flies, this striking action must be modified by the power of the rod and the power the angler applies. A trout of two pounds taking a size 22 dry fly on a 7× leader (testing one pound or less) must be hooked as solidly as a hundred pound tarpon taking a big fly on a stout leader. A great deal of sensitivity on the part of the angler is needed then to adapt to the situation. The rod he uses offers much, if not all of this latitude in striking. The rod acts as a spring, a cushion against his inadequacies and the fish's unaccountable strength at the exact moment of the strike and during the action that follows.

In order to bring about a formula for the angler to follow and use in striking and playing, the allowable positions of the rod during the action should be visualized and known. In order to accomplish this, the exact limitation of the tackle and the precise amount of strain that can be handled before the breaking point of the leader and the breaking or straightening out of the hook must be known.

To find this for the specific tackle being used, rig up the rod, reel, line and leader. String out the line, leader and hook to a solid object some fifty feet from the rod tip. Attach the line to the object and walk away the fifty feet until the line is tight. Now, strike— softly at first, against the line. Add pressure gradually until the full curve of the rod is utilized. In the case of very light leaders such as used in trout fishing, you can strike until you actually break the leader without damaging the rod. Now you know just how much that rig will take in striking force and also its strength in playing power. Remember the pressure you are exerting; look at the bend in the rod and remember it. When performing this experiment with saltwater gear and a heavy leader, do not strike until the heavy leader breaks. Chances are that the rod might go first! But, again, remember the strain possible and the picture of the bent rod during the trial. Those are the limits to remember, even though they will not always be reached in actual fishing.

In this practice, note the POSITION of the rod during the striking and playing action. If the fish were to take the fly while the rod is down parallel to the water, the ENTIRE strain would be directly on the line and leader and the fish would likely break the leader before your reaction and movement to set the hook could engage him. Therefore, when fishing and retrieving the fly do not hold the rod level to the water in DIRECT LINE WITH THE FLY. If you want to keep the rod down, turn it to a right angle to the line so that the fish's strike or the striking move of the rod hand will bring into play the entire rod and its cushioning effect. The same value of spring is accomplished by holding the rod in an almost upright position, the position usually employed when retrieving the fly through the water.

There is the danger of holding the rod too far back, also. If this is done, where could you next move it for more strength? Also, with the rod in a too far back position, most of the backbone of the rod will have been used up and the resultant strain on the line and leader will be too great. So a position somewhere in between is desired. (Figure 5–1)

In the case of small fish and playing the fish, a second cushion is the line in the line hand as it comes from the reel. Here, the angler can either pull in line from the first guide or release it from whatever coils of slack he happens to be holding from a previous retrieve, or he can release it directly from the reel. In the case of handling a big fish, the play comes directly from the reel, itself. The drag on the reel, of course, will have been pre-set to a point well below the breaking point of the leader. In turn this should have been derived from notes and experiments covering the maximum allowable strain on the rod (as performed and recorded through dry run tests). If the brake is set too light, the resultant strike action by the rod hand and the rod will not affect the fish, but will merely pull line from the reel, possibly forming a backlash, and the hook will not be set deeply enough, if at all. If, in striking from the reel, the line is set too tightly, something has got to give, especially when setting a hook in a fish with a soft mouth

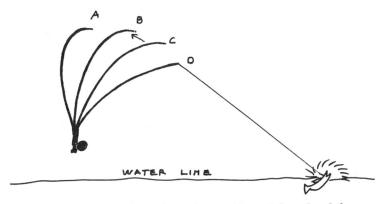

Figure 5-1. This figure shows the various positions of the rod and the way it would bend while striking, playing and landing a fish.

STRIKING: The position D is much too low, allowing the rod to be too straight—too much in line with the line, placing an undue strain on the leader and hook. The fish would tear free or break the line on a savage strike. Position A is much too far back, since in order to hook the fish, the rod would have to be yanked farther back from a position already awkward for the angler. Position C is correct and a good compromise, with the striking action finishing at B.

such as the shad. But once the reel is adjusted properly and the action and power of the rod is known, the angler can go ahead with confidence in setting the hook and playing the fish within the limits set by his brake adjustment and the strength of his tackle combination.

NETTING OR LANDING

Assume now the battle with the fish is being fought at close quarters. Everything is intensified as the angler endeavors to synchronize the response of his tackle and muscles to the struggles of the fish.

The margin for error has increased unless the fish is all but exhausted and is being literally dragged in to the net or the beach.

Quite often, in the case of bass, pike and many of the stronger saltwater fish, they will have the tendency to come in easy only to explode again into action at closer sight of the net and the angler's movements.

It is assumed that as the fish has been brought in, the slack or loose line has been either gathered in coils or reeled back in or perhaps both. A comfortable cushion of extra line should be held in the hand, even if the fish has been played directly from the reel for it is necessary to drop that line fast if the fish makes a sudden run when close to the net. Again rod position and bend is important, and the position should be one which is not awkward to the angler, not too far back, not too much forward; the rod can be held either flat to the water yet at right angles to the line, or upright and fully bent to the strain below.

This is the point where patience is needed. Landing or attempting to land a fish prematurely can end in a bust. Take time and care, bring him in gently and easily, allowing for several runs out if events so dictate. But always keep the line fairly taut and the rod in full spring as the cushion.

When landing the fish in moving water, it is best to get down current from the fish and drop the fish down into the net rather than try to hoist him against the current, thereby adding undue strain, particularly when using light leaders and weak hooks. Do not swipe at the fish as if playing tennis with it, but rather submerge the net and lead the fish into it. Do not move the net, but move the *fish*. This is the trick that many anglers fail to grasp in the all-important seconds before the fish is securely in the meshing. Keep a margin of slack line in the rod hand, just in case of a miss or a slip, or a sudden last lunge by the fish. That slack line in reserve, even though it's short, must be instantly available and the rod kept bent slightly, allowing springy action.

Only once the fish is headed into the net can the scooping be done on a RELAXED line. The fish must have enough line to jump or thrash and enough so he can slip deep into the meshes. On a tight line, however, the fish can swim right out.

In hand landing a fish, particularly those which are to be released, the technique to follow is to stay quietly calm throughout the last minute of play. There is seldom any second chance of

Figure 5-2. In playing the fish, "Hold that rod up!" is the standard advice, not too far back and certainly not too far forward. In LANDING the fish, again, an even tension, utilizing the entire rod's power, cushioning strength and resiliency is required for those last minute sudden lunges of the fish.

Note: This diagram shows the rod in the UP position. Striking, playing and landing can also be done with the same angles of power with the rod held parallel to the water. The only danger in this is that the line is often not held high enough up off the water to keep it free from snags. This is especially something to watch for in bonefishing, Atlantic salmon fishing and when fishing for trout in streams that are full of snags.

bringing the fish into the hand for a release since the fish will bolt at the touch of the hand, and in the interest of his survival, no one wants to tear him loose! Landing the fish to be released can be accomplished by either reaching down the leader until the terminal tackle is felt, and then gently extracting the hook by twisting slightly without ever touching the fish. In the case of the well hooked fish, one hooked deep in the mouth, the fish will have to be firmly hand held while the hook extraction is done. With the free hand in the water, fingers and thumb extended into an open position, the fish is lead into the hand and then grasped lightly behind the gills but without squeezing its stomach. The fish is then held off the water and the hook worked loose or the leader cut just at the knot. The hook will rot out in a few days due to the strong saliva and rusting that will take place. It is sometimes far better to cut the hook off rather than try to extricate it, thereby risking damaging the fish unduly.

When a fish is released it should not merely be dropped back into the water, but gently held in an upright position and allowed to swim out and away from the hand. Select a quiet water section so that the fish can rest there for a while before taking off into the fast water. Remember it is quite exhausted after such an ordeal and will require some time before regaining its strength.

If it is desired to release the netted fish, it is best to try and jiggle the hook loose while the fish is resting in the net. The fish can then be lifted out and the mentioned procedures followed. But be careful, that fish may strike again some day.

6

~~~~~~

Calendar-Related Techniques and Strategies

WHILE TROUT ARE not always opportunistic feeders, the kind of food available to them will vary between Opening Day and the last day of open season. Their feeding habits will also change with fluctuations in water conditions and changes in weather. As the calendar advances, the fly fisherman will therefore try to match his strategy and methods to those which best seem to suit trout during the particular season.

OPENING DAY AND EARLY SEASON TECHNIQUES

Literally hundreds of thousands of freshwater anglers look forward during the long winter months to the first day of the trout season. They tie flies, buy tackle after window shopping, going to

sportsman's shows and attending the club meetings that always
seem to have high interest just before the action starts.

As the days grow shorter, they assemble their gear and break it
down again, waving rods at imaginary targets, testing lines, tying
leaders and placing their tackle in the right pockets of the wading
jacket. Flies are arranged in proper boxes.

NOW!

The magic date is usually in April in the northeast and central
states and across the northern states trout belt to Oregon and
Washington. The opening date is set usually after the snow run-offs
have disappeared and the streams have begun to settle down.
Trout, fresh from the hatcheries, have now had at least a month to
get used to their surroundings and to learn to fend for themselves.

Dawn of the first day finds many anglers heading for the nearest
river, creek, stream or lake, and each weekend for the next month
or two, will find many cars parked along streamsides, near bridges
that cross favorite waters and at the lake shore boat liveries.
Crowds; but it can be a lot of fun and there will be many fish
taken by those who know the rudiments of the game.

Fishing conditions? Rough, generally. A typical opening day
trout stream runs a foot or so high of its normal banks. The water
is cloudy with some snow run-off possible if the preceding weeks
have been frigid. The water temperature is somewhat between 38
and 45 degrees. This means that both the trout and the insects and
baitfish upon which they feed will be relatively inactive in comparison to what they will be like when the temperature rises above 50
degrees. The worm fishermen are favored at this time, since there
is so much earth run-off all along the stream. The thawing earth is
opening up for springtime and worms and bugs and larvae are
being washed into the stream constantly. Wet flies fished in a
drifting manner right along the stream edge, right in among the
willows and stream brush will find trout, as effectively as bait.

Since there will be many anglers wading the river, walking
along the banks and everybody casting, it is good practice to allow
fellow anglers ample room for their sport. There will be spin-
fishermen casting their lures and baits, devout worm fishermen
using either fly fishing or spinning gear and fly fishermen casting

their choice of wet flies, nymphs, streamers and bucktails. A few hardy dry-fly purists may be about with their floating flies. All, or almost all, will catch fish.

The best technique for the fly fisherman is the use of the sinking fly, be it a wet fly, nymph or streamer. The trout will not be actively feeding on or near the surface nor on floating or surface hatching insects. If they are not scared down by all the activity, they will still not be moving about too much. This means getting the fly down to them—actually casting it so that it will be pulled under and down by the current to the bottom of the run or pool being fished. The fly must look like "live" food. This could be nymphs and larvae swimming about the bottom, dislodged nymphs drifting near the bottom or small bait minnows such as dace, shiners and even small trout fry.

April means rain, heavy showers and gusty winds. Fly casting is made more difficult so short casts are in order. Line can be paid out in downstream casting, once the fly has been laid on the water. This added slack line will allow the fly to sink, drifting over likely spots on its way downstream. The across and downstream cast is advised. As the fly drifts down, it will reach the end of the line allowed and will circle in toward the bank or directly below the angler if he is wading. It is then retrieved to be cast again and again. This action simulates the dead drift of an imitated insect, be it a nymph, larva or dead insect that has fallen into the water from upstream.

The active form of fly fishing utilizes the bucktail or streamer that is designed to imitate a stream minnow. During the drift the fly is twitched by rod tip jerking so that the fly becomes alive during its drift downstream. It is then actively retrieved in short jerks back upstream before the recast.

In order to sink these flies effectively in high, roily and deep pool water, it is advisable to attach split-shot onto the leader, or wind on flat lead strips ahead of the fly or flies.

There are times and situations when wet flies are effectively fished right on the surface, even in the early part of the season. Often trout will rise to flies that are dappled and skittered over the surface.

The early season is not without some kind of a hatch unless the air and water temperature are extremely low. This means the possibility of a sizable hatch and therefore the use of the dry fly, especially if trout are seen rising to the insects.

It is quite possible to start in the early morning with, say, the streamer fly fished deep. If the sun comes out and the air warms up a trifle, a possible hatch will come off later, just after noon. About ten or eleven o'clock nymphs may be seen drifting in the current and a sharp eye will find the trout feeding on them well down from the surface of the pool or run. When the nymphs reach the surface and begin to cast their nymphal shuck, the trout will be seen bulging and slashing the surface. They are still feeding from a position underwater, so wet flies are in order. But when the trout are actually jumping out and circling over the emerged flies, it is prime time for the dry fly. Thus, the angler can have, in the space of a few hours, the complete experience of all basic forms of fly fishing from the bottom to the top.

Opening Day, then, can be full of surprises.

And those hatchery trout will be welcome prizes. There are those so-called sophisticated anglers who look down their noses at freshly planted trout. To be sure, they are not as active, full bodied or as natural feeders as the wild-bred trout, but for most of us, such wild trout are not to be had except in the back country streams or in streams set aside for fly fishing only. These streams need little restocking in comparison with those streams where bait fishing and spin-fishing are popular.

But those hatchery trout will offer much challenge to the angler for they can be very shy and selective as to what they go for. The experts tell us that freshly planted trout will not take a fly readily. This is tommyrot! I've had trout bang into each other in a hatchery pool trying to grab a fly cast to them on a barbless hook!

There will be a great and interesting bit of interchange between fellow anglers during the first days of the season. Everybody seems friendly and glad to be fishing. They'll gladly tell what they caught their fish on or share a technique, particularly with a beginner. Also a beginner can and should do as much watching as fishing. Watching an expert can save many years of trial and error.

One trick to remember is that of getting into the stream below a group of anglers who are fishing above. As they wade about, the stream bottom is disturbed by their boots. The insects are set free from the bottom and drift in the current. The trout below that point see the insects drifting down to them. Place your flies in the current eddies so that they drift naturally right in among the real thing.

Take care in wading in that cloudy water. It is difficult if not impossible to see the bottom after getting in to knee height. Also the currents can be more forceful than they look. One false step into a hole and the current can take the angler for a watery ride.

Spin-fishermen may be seen taking trout when the flies are not delivering. The worm or bait fishermen may be seen taking trout when results with flies are zero. But, remember that the time will come sometime during the day when the flies will really pay off. Many experts will tell you that in the course of a few minutes, during the time the trout were really active they hooked and released their limit, while the bait fishermen and spin-fishermen watched from the sidelines, their mouths wide open with amazement.

Trout fishing in the lakes during the early spring can be a very touchy proposition. On many lakes the trout feed on the surface for only a few days or at the most three weeks. Then they go down deep and stay there for the balance of the season. (See Chapter 7.) When they are up on the surface, fly fishing will take them over all other forms of fishing. If the angler were to spin-cast a heavy spoon lure, he'd scare the trout half to death. The worm fisherman cannot cast his bait far enough and even if he could, the splash would put the fish off feed. The fly fisherman making very long casts with light long leaders equipped with a tiny fly similar to those on the surface can take trout, sometimes very big ones, with comparative ease.

In lake or stream, the early season doesn't demand getting out on the water in the damp of dawn or trying to fish in the cold late afternoon. It is too cold for both the angler and the trout. The best time to be abroad is in the middle of the day, when, hopefully, the wind will not be too harsh on the cheek or make casting a hardship.

One of the best times of the year is the opener. That first trout caught on a fly the angler has tied himself is a triumph!

MIDSEASON FLY FISHING

The stream is more defined now, the water levels are down to near normal or, in some cases, if the spring rains have subsided, the levels are even lower than normal. What was a raging torrent of rushing, discolored water is now a series of divided currents of clear water. The bottom of the stream can be seen even at the deepest parts. The temperature of the water is now above the 50 degree mark which spells the time for the insect hatches to proceed along their regular schedule. Mayflies, caddis flies, crane flies, fish flies, stone flies plus the myriad of land-bred insects will be seen on or in the water.

The smart angler will be abroad over a greater hour span—from early morning to late into the twilight and his day can be filled with everything from "fish finding" with bucktails and streamers or wet flies and nymphs, for the serious angler wanting to match the hatching activity. The dry fly fisherman, often fishless during the early sessions, will have a distinct advantage over the bait and spin-fishermen. When the flies are hatching, or the Mayfly spinners are abroad at twilight and during the evening rise, they will be able to take a limit of trout—or at least get rises on almost every cast.

Wading will now have to be a bit more careful. Fish can easily be put down, or scared out of the pool or put on the run by careless wading. In fact, many experts prefer to stay ashore, despite the high price they may have paid for good waders. It is better to cast from the shore if and when possible rather than invade the pool, making obvious waves and wakes.

This calls for expert casting ability, or at least the ability to get a longer line out than was needed in the early days of the year. Leaders will have to be longer and flies should be selected with an eye to the insects abroad. Streamers and bucktails can be a little smaller—and if you tie your own—sparser in dressing so that they will sink easier and make less of a splash on the water. Angles of

presentation should be studied. It is not necessary to cast indis-
criminantly all over the pool, just get the fly in the water. It is
more like a billiard game now. Call the shots.

When fishing a small creek, stay on the bank and dapple the
flies right at your feet, along the undercut banks, into the deep
holes under overhanging trees, behind rocks and into the deep
runs where the stream bends and makes shallows and deeps. Fish
upstream so that the trout are not scared by the approach. They
are headed into the current, remember, so they do not see you too
well from behind.

When fishing a big, broad river, remember that the big water
need not tempt the angler to merely cover the water. A big river in
fact is nothing but a collection of little streams. The fish are not
necessarily always in the deepest parts. When it is considered how
many trout are caught in the shallower parts of a little creek it is
evidence that those same trout could be taken in water that is just
as shallow if in a big river—to the sides, along the edges, in the
ruts and runs in the tails of pools.

Before beginning to fish, look over the water carefully. In a
pool or deeper stretch, if the light is right, trout can be seen often
nosing the bottom for caddis flies and other aquatic nymphs and
larvae. With no hatch in progress, they will feed on the generous
fare found on the stream bottom. In the early morning, wet flies
can be used since many of the insects that have hatched miles
above are still drifting on the current. Also, the bucktail and
streamer are good since the minnows are active now and trout
love a meal of such fare.

Unless there are indications of a hatch, dry-fly fishing, if that
method is preferred by the angler, can be productive too. Even
though it makes no sense to fish with dry flies because of a lack of
surface insects, it is possible and probably true more often than
not that trout still can be enticed to the surface. This is really the
prime attraction of dry fly fishing—the idea of "bring 'em up." It
doesn't always work, but when it does it makes the hours of
fishless casting worth while.

It is possible now to cause them to surface, because at this time
they are becoming increasingly interested in what goes on on the

surface anyway. In the early days of the season they don't even look towards the surface, but by mid-season or a little later, they begin to cock their eyes upwards. Even in the bright light of day a trout will sometimes rise to a dainty dry fly, deftly handled drag-free on the surface. If there is a calm stretch of pool water and a little breeze is ruffling the surface, a skater, or spider fly is good medicine. It acts like an escaping or hatching insect and seems to bring out the cat-and-mouse in almost every creature. If it looks like it is going to escape into the air, the trout will automatically want it.

The serious nymph fisherman who has been fishing the streams in the general area or a specific stream for several years, knows what insects are hatching at a specific time of the month and season. He also knows the temperature needed for the eventual hatch. He can start out by fishing a specific nymph type, down deep, wet-fly sunken style during the morning and gradually fish higher up during the afternoon. By observing the water at his side, the insects can be seen drifting in the current. A smart eye will see trout rolling for the insects well under the surface. Out in the center of a quiet stretch of water on a big pool, trout will be seen "hanging" in the current, almost upright in the current. Big ones, too! Don't wade in here. Stay as far away as possible, or if you have approached by wading into such an area move into casting position VERY SLOWLY, foot by foot, inching toward the spot where you can preferably cast the fly from an angle rather than directly upstream, since the leader will not then drift down over them before they can see the fly. They are touchy in this position, and should be cast to with utmost caution. Brown trout will be found in this position and once in a while rainbows. Brook trout will hardly ever be found in this situation, since they do not prefer the open water—at least the bigger ones that are the prime attraction.

As to fly choice, it is always advisable to fish the smallest fly you can tie on. The fly makes less of a bounce on the cast, and offers less chance to be refused if the trout are finicky or selective. When a particular hatch of Mayflies, for example, are on the water and the trout are nosing around under them, a fly of larger size will tend to scare them down, or invite a refusal. Our man-made imitations, at best are far from the real thing, so use a smaller imitation. Make the trout a bit curious, even if the fly doesn't exactly remind them of the real thing.

The direct opposite of this is often recommended. If it seems to be impossible to lure trout to your little artificial during the times when the flies are drifting and the trout are bulging the surface for them, go completely unorthodox. Shoot 'em a Royal Coachman Fanwing. This ruse often works. Maybe the trout think that the big fly is a land-bred drop in and, if it looks succulent, they'll often fall for it.

The late afternoon and early evening are the prime times for the fly fisherman during the midseason. Most of the hatches will be coming on as the sun begins to lower and the shadows lengthen over the water. Also, the spinners or adult versions of the Mayfly duns will be coming out of the woods, from the brush along the streams or from the banks that are grassy and rocky. They mate in the air over the stream. Quickly, the eggs mature in the female and then the fishing action starts. It will be signaled by the advance flights of kingbirds, swallows and phoebes over the water. They, too, like the feed coming up. The water temperature has given the signal for the nymphs to hatch from below. The surface of the water is then getting its tempting fare from both directions and the trout like this. They feed almost indiscriminately once the rush is on. Almost any dry fly aptly presented will get a rise.

Wet flies, skittered over the surface at the head of a run, along a shelving riffle, along a drop-off, or along the edges of the head of a pool will draw results. Keep an eye on the action and see where the trout are congregating. Do not cast the flies right over the fish. This will put them down for sure. Remember that the imitations are not exact, no matter how well they are made and the directly cast line and leader can spell doom to the situation. Cast rather to the side of the action, along the edges of the currents that are carrying the drifting insects. The trout will see the fly; don't worry about that. Cast from an angle across rather than directly up-stream, as stated before, and pick your casts with care instead of merely flipping the flies out there just anywhere at all.

The heads of pools are likely spots for this action, but do not neglect the tail of the pool where it begins to shallow out, for here the big trout begin to come forth from the hiding places and work their way upstream from their daytime holding positions. The evening rise can be the most potent time for the fly fisherman.

When it is almost dark, the fly fishing on the surface, at least, will begin to fall off. The trout have been gorging themselves for at least an hour and are well satiated. They will now become highly selective and the action seen a few hours before will have all but diminished.

But this is the time that the big trout come up for the first time of the day. Quality will replace quantity. The smaller fish will not like to be around the bigger ones.

The light is bad, and it is difficult to see the fly on the water. Use one with a white wing, or a wisp of white, such as the bivisible, or a white hairwing dry fly. Pattern now is of little importance. Careful and restricted casting is, however. Try and locate a big trout that is consistently feeding at the same location and approach him with caution, casting and drifting the fly, letting the area rest a while before recasting.

Night fishing is the next step and this is an art, all by itself in the realms of angling.

NIGHT FLY FISHING

This is a sport all its own, demanding certain and special desires, talents and actions. It is not for everybody.

To fully understand night fishing, the right conditions must be known and met.

The dark of the moon is the best time. This means that the angler must be able to find his way through brush, rocks and streamside hazards even before he enters the water. He must be able to tie all the necessary knots as if blind. No lights, not even a flashlight or cigarette lighter once near or on the water. He'll have to be able to cast well enough to get forty feet of line out on the water and sense the background trees and snags so that he will not cast into them by mistake. The roll cast is out—too much water disturbance.

If the angler is in a hurry—stay home. Even the approach to the night fishing spot must be slow. The night spells stillness. Every pounding step will be felt out there in the water, and once in the water the crunching of gravel and rocks underfoot are danger signals to the trout. So each step must be soft, unhurried and the wading kept to a minimum.

Casts will be few and far between, but those casts that are made will be productive. The retrieve of the line will not be the familiar "whoosh-type" used during the daytime. The fly will have to be retrieved slowly back almost to under the rod tip before the next cast is made.

There are good and valid reasons for all of this special care.

The trout to be fished over will only be the big ones. The little fish will be napping. Every good trout stream harbors big trout, but daytime anglers hardly ever see them, for too much wading and casting will keep them down deep or in hiding. Big trout simply will not put up with all that foolishness.

The reason why those trout are big is because they're survived perhaps four or five years since their initial planting in the stream, perhaps even more years if they were naturally spawned in upper tributaries. They are the monsters of the stream—big fish that eat their weight in other trout in a week.

They used to feed at almost any time during the early season, but now their forays are strictly limited to the late evenings or in the deep of night.

They move out from their lairs slowly. At times they can be detected beginning to feed, generally in mid-stream over a deep section as the last light disappears. During the warmer evenings when it takes more time for the water surface to cool, they may not come out until ten or even eleven o'clock.

When they do, they take up a position a few yards below the rock breaks at the head of a pool. It is difficult to spot them or hear them feeding. At other times they take station at the center of the pool, where the current is not quite so fast, but where the current collides in a lane that collects the night flying insects such as the stone flies and the myriad of land-breds, including big moths and millers.

Out there it is possible to spot a lunker. His snout may be all you may see, or his dorsal fin, or possibly—if in the action of busting water over a bug—his broad tail. That's the fish to be after. No trial casting here. Wait ashore to see the start of a big fish feeding and then go after him. If there are others, all well and good. It does little good to merely cast hoping that a big trout is out there. If he's there it will be known as the eyes become accustomed to the pitch dark.

Before entering the water or making that first cast, the angle of fly presentation should be considered. Perhaps only one or four casts at the most will be made over that fish. Too many casts will put him (and the other trout) off feed, perhaps for the night.

The best angle is *not* directly upstream, even with the dry fly. Quarter across the stream, in an upstream direction, which will allow casting the fly to a couple of yards above the feeder. The fly will then drift down over him with the leader to the side. By placing the fly in the current drift with the other insects, he'll see it—no matter.

If the trout is actually actively feeding, he'll come up and slurp the surface with his mouth. There is no sound quite like it and it is an unmistakable sign that he means business.

Best dry flies for night fishing are large and overdressed to float well and offer a large silhouette. Some night fishermen even use very small bass bugs. The Wulff flies with the large and full hackle and hair wings are excellent. These should be tied with white wings for, believe it or not, out there in the pitch black there is often enough light to make them shine a little.

Do not cast the fly directly over a feeding fish. Cast it to the side, let it drift down well below him before you begin to make the retrieve. Often during this retrieve, when the fly is approaching the edge of the stream, it is possible to pick up a trout that was not spotted as a feeder, so work the fly back to the rod tip as mentioned earlier. Then wait until you see the trout resume feeding, or until one or two others can be spotted near him doing the same thing.

Trout are more active during the nights when the aquatic stone flies are hatching. These flies do not hatch in the midstream or even along the centers of pools. They crawl out on the rocks to cast their shucks and emerge as adult flying insects. They sometimes hatch in great quantities. It is on those evenings that night fishing can be most exciting. Those empty shucks seen during the day are mute evidence.

Since they hatch along the partially wet rocks, gravel and sand, this means that the trout will come into the shallows after them. Again, standing back from the stream, this action can be seen. Often a cast where most of the line will rest on the rocks and gravel with only the leader and fly landing just off into the water will get action.

Generally the strike of a night feeding fish is not dramatic. He's just waiting there, opening his mouth as a succulent insect drifts by. He can reject that fly the instant it touches him if he detects the fraud. Another reason why a fully dressed fly is better.

But once that trout heads down with the fly in its mouth, the action starts. Stay ashore if you possibly can, for after the disturbance made by the fighting fish, the pool will settle down and the other trout will begin feeding again.

Try and lead the fish downstream from where the action of feeding has been going on so that a second chance in that pool can be had.

Wade carefully. It is always a good plan to have waded that same water during the daytime before the night foray, making mental notes as to the amount of backcast room available, the deep holes and places to avoid when wading. A knowledge of the currents and the flow of daytime insects along the lanes should be noted, for the night insects take the same trip and the trout wait there for them.

If the water fished is a good way from the road, mark the paths well to and from. Also, it is best to let somebody know where you are and when you'll be back. It is possible to slip and fall into trouble. But the prizes to be taken are large and well worth the exercise.

LATE SEASON FISHING

The weather is hot. Midsummer doldrums—dog days over most of the trout belt. Even in the high mountain areas the weather is extremely hot and bright. The water levels are well down from the normal heights. The water temperatures in many streams approach the uncomfortable degrees above seventy that makes both the insect life and the trout loggish. With higher temperatures, the water contains less oxygen and the trout become congregated in the areas of the stream that afford a combination of shadows and protection and fresh air to breathe. This changeover from even the end of mid-season must be taken into consideration by the angler. There are a lot of areas in even a big river that are devoid of fish during the day.

Trout will be found at the heads of pools, down under the white water where there is comparatively little current to fight against constantly. They will also be found in bubbly runs by drop-offs and curiously enough in shallow water where it is rushing by rocks and gravel. They will not seek out (unless disturbed by wading and over-fishing) the deepest parts of the pool.

Early morning, preferably just at dawn, will find them out for their breakfast. They'll take wet flies dappled across the surface or dead drifted in the feed lanes, since many of the insects in the late season diet are drop-ins from the night before. Bucktails and streamers cast into and across the bubbly and surfy stretches of white water *and allowed to be fished deep* will take summer trout in the morning.

In the middle of the day the trout will sleep it out, usually in the comforting shade of a mid-stream rock, an old dead tree trunk along the stream bank where the current affords a deep trench, or under the protective crosscurrents that make spotting them from the sky all but impossible. At times it is possible to spot a trout lying right on the bottom near a rock and to wade up to it and poke it with the rod tip to dislodge it. A short while later the fish will return to its lair and go back to resting it out until evening.

Those summer trout are hard to catch whether the angler goes after them with shiny spinning lures, choice red worms or the best of flies.

But they can be brought into action if, and only if, all the qualities needed for night fishing are recognized. Longer casts, lighter leaders, smaller flies, not-too-much casting but more strategic casting and drifting. Strangely enough, a sunken fly will sometimes do better than a floater, particularly if no insects are on the surface to attract their attention. Often a brace of two very small wet flies allowed to drift a foot under the surface, somewhat like they are employed in the early season, will get better results.

A wide look at a given stretch of water or a long glassy pool will reveal every stone and pebble on the bottom. A closeup through binoculars will sometimes reveal some trout, but all of them will be lying still. Once in a while a little trout will bounce up for a butterfly or other land-bred insect that's making a tiny fuss on the water. The minnows will be active in this way too and, if lucky, the angler will spot a big trout taking off after him. But these times are exceptions.

Evening is another story. After the surface water has cooled, even a very few degrees, activity is sponsored by the elements. Usually late afternoon breezes come up, ruffling the surface, blowing in insects from the nearby fields and trees. This starts the action even though there is little, if any, nymphal activity and no hatches are present or called for in the schedule.

One of the most interesting hatches during the late season is the midge. This tiny fly, represented by a size 20 or smaller dry fly, imitates the midge larvae about to hatch on the surface. When one of the midge hatches develops, it hatches in droves. Thousands of the insects will rise from the bottom of the stream in a big mad rush and all of them will reach the surface at about the same time. As the insects drift down the current lanes, they become crowded into a steady stream of goodies for the trout. This activity pulls the trout to attention and they will move out, at first with some caution and then, with the large amount of the insects at their disposal, they will literally gorge themselves with utter abandon.

The way to these trout is simple, yet it requires tackle to suit the moment. The flies are small and require very thin leader tippets, 7× at the most. A leader tippet of about two feet should be tied to the end of a 9 foot leader tapered to four ×. The light 7×

will be limp to cast, but will afford sufficient slack to allow the fly to drift more naturally in or on the current. Properly fished, the fly does not sit up right as a conventional dry fly would do, but it sits hook-down on the surface. In this position, under the distractions of light refraction and reflections, the fly is difficult to see and follow as it drifts over the feeding trout. The end of the leader where it joins the fly line is the only "bobber" to be used in this fishing. Watch that end of the line for any sudden movement thought to be the strike of a trout. There will be a lot of misses, since the trout can and do reject these flies very easily. Also, there will be minnows and small trout taking them and the angler will never know which, or whether the slight twitch of the line will signal a good sized trout.

The other alternative to taking summer trout in the daytime is the use of land-bred insect imitations. Among the greats are any flies that approximate the grasshopper. The same fly looks also like the stonefly that sometimes hatches in late summer, so the chances of fish catching with a big fly are theoretically doubled in the logic of this imitation. These together with the aforementioned spider flies are "fish finders" that most of the experts rely on during the day and into the evening hours.

The best approach to the pool to be fished is to start at the bottom and wade in quietly and fish slowly up the pool, making sure and direct casts to allow the flies to drift in the feed lanes and converging currents. Any mid-stream rocks or snags, or even shallow gravel bars should be washed by the casts. Rather than fan out with the casts—putting them side by side—it is better to spot-cast in one direction and then put the next cast in an entirely different location, resting the area in case a trout was scared down by the slapping line. On another cast in the same general direction he just may come up to take a look at the fly.

Late season angling is a time for experimentation. Keep an eye on the water for any constant type of blow-in land-bred fly. Sometimes, for example, a whole flight of ants will descend on the river. The trout love them and will immediately gorge themselves while the supply lasts and then just as quickly settle back for their snooze.

A sudden change of wind, a lowering or upping of the barometer or the signs of a coming thunderstorm will trigger changes underwater. It is up to the angler to be observant and try to use the changes to his advantage.

After the sunset—then it's night fishing for sure.

SOME SAMPLE STREAM FISHING PROBLEMS

The several stream situations in the accompanying diagrams are an exercise in observation and strategy. Where to wade, where to cast and retrieve the flies and the probable places where the fish will be resting or feeding (sometimes quite different locations). Note the code for the diagrams and they will be easy to read and study. Next time you go fishing you'll remember them.

Figure 6-1. An overall look at this stretch of stream reveals three definite clusters of rocks. Each takes a different casting position and coverage for the proper line presentation for needed fly drifts and retrieves. Note that on this 75 foot wide pool, little or no wading is necessary. Ordinarily, anglers will wade right up through the pool, disturbing all the hot spots. Fish it from the shore, as near to the shore as possible, for casting ease and back-cast room.

Fishing upstream from (1), upstream casts starting at (2) and fanning over to the four center rocks is good for all flies, wets, nymphs, streamers and dry flies. These feed lanes of broken water hold trout. A better angle at the rocks is from position (2) and, if necessary, make rollcasts unless you can wade out a bit from shore. At (3) it is possible to cast downstream to a position between (1) and (10), working up to casting in between the rocks and even above them. Work the two center rocks without moving. At (4) downstream casting to (2) and out to the center rocks is potent for bucktails and downstream nymphing. It also provides a long upstream and cross dry fly cast to the wash below the single center rock. (5) and (6) offer double chances at the dead currents in front of the rock and below it, as do (7) and (8). (9) is the position for downstream and across, working the two center rocks and the heads of the four rocks below. At (10) the rock washes and rushing water at the tail of the section can be worked by across and downstream casts.

Notice how much fishing there is to be had in this short stretch of water. Note how little wading is necessary. All methods can be employed, from bottom dredging with nymphs to bucktails fished up and down, to wet fly fishing across and up and down, and dry fly fishing both up and down. Properly fished, this section should take at least four hours of careful fishing to completely exhaust it.

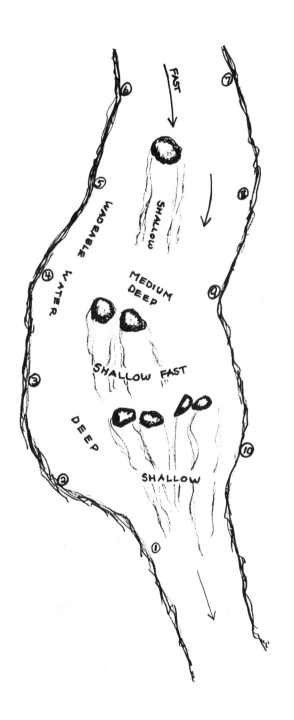

Figure 6-2.   Before entering the water at (1) study the layout and plot the course to be followed. There is little need to wade except in the last stages. All kinds of water here, and the head of a pool harbors large fish. At (1), up and across wet fly and dry fly fishing is done by fanning out the casts to as far as (12) and across to (13). At (2)—a variation of angle and possibly good for across stream and drift-down bucktails. At (3) fish short dappling casts to the break in the gravel, reach out to (12) with some bucktails that will sink into the deep slow below. At (4) cast downstream through the shallows with nymphs and even dry flies and shoot some dry flies to the two rocks above that position.

Wade out in the shallow gravel, working dry flies into the fast deep and then try wet flies and nymphs, working the same area thoroughly with sunken bucktails—all from the same position. Position (5) allows working over the fast deep water and casts to the rocks at the head of the pool off of (6). At (6) the entire top of the pool with its broken runs can be worked, particularly with bucktails, allowing the flies to circle and drift through the broken shallows off (8).

Rather than wade in at (8) go down to (9) and wade over to (10), casting both up and down as you go. The casts to (11) and (12) are potent for wet flies and dry flies during a hatch. At (11) work the top of the pool with drys and downstream with wets and nymphs. Dropping down to (12) you have the entire lower half of the pool for downstream set, nymph and streamer fishing. Quite a day of shifting from one method to another, observing the water currents, shallows, deep runs and holding water for trout.

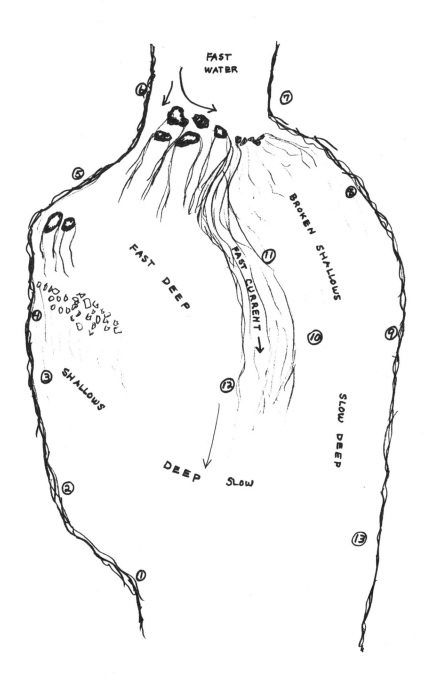

Figure 6-3. The tail of the pool is just as potent and in some cases more potent than the head of a pool, since many of the trout drop down to the easier water. Since more fishermen fish the head, the tail is left alone and the trout like it that way.

Following along what has been shown in the preceding figures, start fishing upstream from (1) and (2) working all methods before moving along. There is no hurry. There's enough fishing from (1) to (4) to keep one busy for an hour and slow wading and walking will not put the fish down. (4) and (5) are potent for covering everything to the deep center run and all the way to (6) with a possible wade out to (7) which affords all methods ample experimentation.

Working the section from the other side at (8), that deep fast run below is fine for nymphing with weighted nymphs. The broken shallows can be combed with dappled spider dry flies and wets. (9), (10) and (11) will take a good two hours to exhaust even with only a few well placed casts, depending on the types of flies being used.

One of the best times to work this section is in the late twilight during the midseason when insects are hatching above and the fish are rising. Work the deep fast run and the medium deep run especially, since the main flow of insects will be coming right down the street.

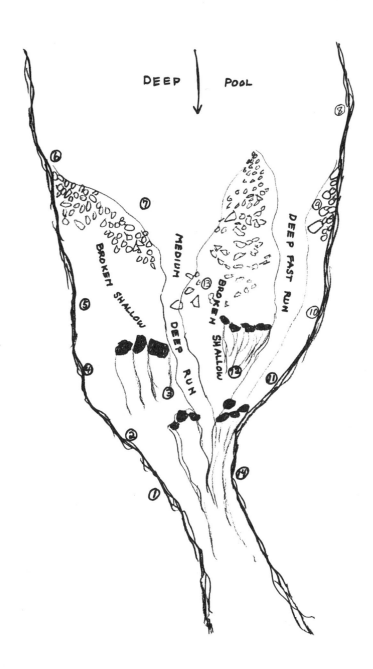

DEEP ↓ POOL

DEEP FAST RUN

BROKEN SHALLOW

MEDIUM

BROKEN SHALLOW

DEEP RUN

Figure 6-4. Every wave in the stream's course has a shallow and a deep section, due to the curving course. This can be broken and altered slightly by rocks and shallows, but the high waters usually carve their way in this type of pattern. Fish like the holding water and only venture into the fast water when definitely on feed. Work the slower sections by following the numbers on the diagram, wade as little as possible and remember, if you are fishing upstream, to turn around once in a while and cast downstream, even if using the dry fly. If fishing dowstream with wets, nymphs and bucktails, remember to cast upstream once in a while for a generous and deep drift of the flies to well below your position and then retrieve the flies back up to the rod.

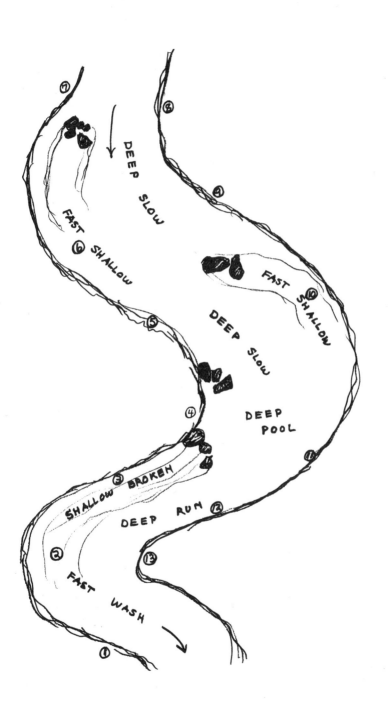

7

Fishing Lakes and Artificial Impoundments

THERE IS NOTHING quite so blank looking as the surface of a lake. It is as flat as a pancake and very mysterious. What's under the surface? How deep is it, where are the deeps, the spring holes, the drop-offs, the ledges, the shallows, the weed beds, the inlets or feeder streams, the outlet, the sharp points of land, the deep indentations, the mid-lake grass flats and shallows? What is the temperature of the surface water? Is this compatible to the fish at this season? At what depth should fly trolling be done? What are the principal baitfish to be imitated by artificial flies and how should they be rigged and fished in trolling and casting? Then—are there any fish in the lake? What species? Where are the hot spots at a given time of the year under certain weather conditions?

All this and more must be known in order to connect with the catch. Secondarily comes the techniques for catching the fish.

FISH ARE THERE—BUT WHERE?

Lake fishing is not nearly as simple as stream fishing, for in the stream natural conditions dictate the fishing hot spots and the techniques for casting to the fish that are lying there or at specific feeding locations. In lake fishing, none of this information is readily known. But it can be discovered in many ways.

One way, of course, is to employ a guide, especially in fishing a lake that is entirely unfamiliar to the angler. Another way is to look for a map of the lake and its hot spots—sometimes available. Even a simple road map of the territory usually details something of the lake shore, showing the inlets, outlets, tributary streams, major points of indentation, and importantly, ways of access by car or foot. Some also show boat landings, islands, and other features of interest to the fisherman. Often even better is a geodetic map of the area and this should be thoroughly studied and brought along on the trip, safely wrapped against water and spray. With the depths known in advance, it will be fairly simple to locate the *possible* hot spots.

Fish react to water temperature in the same fashion as humans do to air temperature. They move around in the lake, up and down and sideways in order to live in a comfortable temperature. That's why they are found in some sections of a lake at one time and at another spot at another time. At some seasons they are found living and feeding on the surface and at others, hiding deep down. This has to be accepted and reckoned with.

Then there is the matter of feed. The gamefish will be where the food and baitfish are located. This circumstance can change by the hour. A sudden alteration in the climate conditions from rain today, hot to cold, or from cold to hot, or a serious drop or rise in the barometer can quickly and definitely alter all conditions. Merely casting hour after hour and traversing the shorelines, deeps and shallows could be a waste of time regardless of the techniques used and mastery of tackle and gear.

In order for the angler to not completely miss the "luck" he deserves, or to merely bump into the good fishing on a few occasions during his possibly expensive stay at the lake, there are many constants upon which he can depend. In addition, the guide or the locals who will advise him from shore if he takes off in a boat alone to fish, know much of this information and can give it to him freely if he will listen.

The specific fish species must be known from study and accumulated past experience. Landlocked salmon and brook trout in the lakes of northern Maine and New Brunswick react to their homes in a much different way than the big largemouths of a Florida lake. The smallmouth bass of a Lake-of-the-Woods pond in Ontario don't live the same as those in Dale Hollow and the TVA lakes of Tennessee and Kentucky.

In order to enjoy excellent topwater fly casting and surface trolling for landlocked salmon, the angler has to be right on the spot just as the ice goes out from the lakes. There's a period then, when the smelt are running to their spawning streams and shore locations, when the landlocks can be taken in numbers by casting streamers and wet flies and even dry flies. But the minute the water surface warms up, they go deeper and deeper. In a matter of two weeks' time they can be taken from the top and then to a depth of ten feet or more. Same for the brook trout. Rainbow trout in the colder lakes in the northern states react somewhat the same, rising to flies in the first days and weeks of the season. Cutthroats in a Washington State lake may be found along the shoreline in early season but will quickly center in the deeper water leaving the shoreline to the bass for the remainder of the season. It is then a matter of trolling over the cooler spots, spring holes and stream entries—specific locations—rather than merely casing the lake by hours of fruitless casting and trolling.

Brown trout also react varyingly to weather conditions and water temperatures, although they can stand warmer water than brook or rainbow trout. But they too have their day on the surface, to go down deep to join the lake trout in the cooler bands of water in a given lake.

Then, there are various kinds of lakes—the shallow lakes and ponds and the deeper lakes and particularly the artificial impoundments and reservoirs. While these artificial lakes require a special kind of study, the fish react according to their needs.

A knowledge of the particular baitfish to be imitated by the artificial flies is needed. Local guides, outfitters and fly tiers have spent many years in developing both standard patterns and special innovations that will catch fish under specific conditions on a specific lake or chain of lakes. Mark their advice and get those patterns. Also heed their recommended techniques for casting and trolling these flies.

In bass fishing, there is quite a bit of difference in the habits of smallmouth bass and largemouths in a given lake at specific times. The largemouth bass is more likely to put up with warmer temperatures and seek out warmer water than the smallmouth. Usually the largemouth will be found in the shallower waters and along the lake shore in contrast to the smallmouth, particularly in the early part of the season. When the water gets too warm along the edges, even the largemouth will seek out the depths and join the smallmouth and lake trout.

Even during a twenty-four hour period much movement can be charted for game fish, depending on the season, barometer, water temperature and baitfish conditions.

LAKE FISH AND FAVORED TEMPERATURES

Regardless of everything else, the study of fish and their preferred temperatures should be made. It has been, by excellent biologists and fisheries experts who depend on this knowledge to help them ascertain just what fish populations are best for the lakes and rivers under their supervision. This information together with actual fishing results can form a basis for ascertaining just where and when to fish for specific varieties.

The panfish, such as bluegills, sunfish, crappies and largemouth bass can stand temperatures of from 65 to 75 and even 80 degrees. Their lakes become much colder than this in the winter in northern zones. At these times they become very dormant, however. At the opposite end of the temperature spectrum is the lake trout and landlocked salmon. They survive best in temperatures from 40–55 degrees and are most active on the surface at this time. When the temperature of the lake rises above this point, they sink down to cooler levels. If it is colder such as in winter, they too, become dormant. Yellow perch, smallmouth bass, pike, muskellunge and pickerel like their homes warmed from 60 to 75 degrees for their most active period, while brown trout and rainbows like it a trifle cooler—somewhere between 45 to 50 up to 70 degrees. The brook trout likes it about ten degrees cooler for optimum action. Again, above and below these ranges, the fish tend to be either inactive or seek out new areas with more compatible temperatures; sometimes moving where fly fishing for them is not feasible.

In lakes in the northern states, these temperatures range from near freezing on the bottom, depending on the depth, to a high of 80 degrees or more in exceptionally hot summer "dog days." The temperatures various species of fish prefer can tell the angler at just what depths to fish for them, or to forget trying to fish for them altogether with flies. The only way to catch them in hot weather is very deep stillfishing.

UNDERSTANDING HOW A LAKE "WORKS"

In northern lakes where the temperatures vary over a wide range, violent changes in the water take place. In winter, when the lake freezes over with ice, a kind of insulation covers the surface and the temperature ranges near freezing just under the "cap." Below this point, strangely enough, the water becomes warmer and more dense until a temperature of about 40 degrees is reached at the bottom. When the ice begins to deteriorate due to the longer period of sunlight reaching it as the spring advances, the ice begins to reach the point of breakup. This can happen in but a day or two and lo, the ice is "out." The lake is clear and breathing again— then comes the spring fishing action!

With the ice now gone from the lake the first phase of its annual change cycle takes place. The warmth from the sun raises the water temperature from near freezing to about 40 degrees. At this point the surface water matches the temperature of the warmer water that before was layered below the ice. Fish therefore come to the surface and range throughout the entire lake depths, since the water layers are nearly all the same. Fish that were dormant during the cold winter now feed with abandon in this period of spring activity.

Now, take into consideration the winds. That wind blowing over the lake should be blowing surface food to the shore, so it would be supposed that this shore ought to be the best to fish. But, if the temperature of water along the on-wind shore is measured it will be found that the water is still too cold there for most fish. The opposite shore would be best because there the water would be a little warmer, a fact proven time and again by guides as well as biologists! So wind action can fool the angler. It can break up the ice prematurely, but it won't bring good fishing until the surface waters are at the proper temperatures.

As spring edges toward summer another change in the lake occurs. The surface water becomes increasingly warmer. This produces lighter water, lighter and warmer than that in layers below. A mixing of warm and cold water takes place forming a third layer of water which drops in temperature sometimes quite quickly. This middle layer can be a shallow band in a shallow lake or a wide band in deeper lakes. It remains at about the same general temperature all summer long and it is there that the fish will be found when the surface water gets too warm. At the same time there is little food deep down in a lake to lure fish there and the lowest water layer is often too cold, so it is not a truism that fishing is always best at the deepest part of the lake. It is better to work the intermediate zones all around the lake shore, the islands, mid-lake shallows, bars and reefs. The spring hole where cold water seeps into the bottom of the lake is only a good fishing locality when sufficient vegetation exists nearby and when the prevailing water temperature is not too low for the species of fish being sought.

The best way to take the temperature of a lake is by lowering a thermometer and holding it for readings of five-foot levels. From the fly fishing point of view casting can, or course, only be done at the surface to the five or ten-foot level. And flies can be trolled down to about ten or fifteen feet without the use of heavy sinkers and lures.

Study the diagram of a composite type of lake that is designed

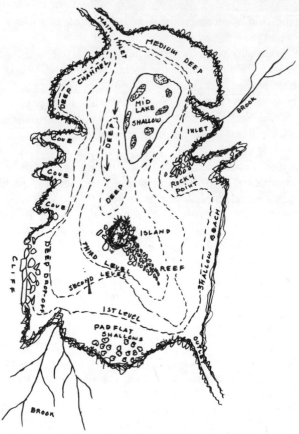

Figure 7-1. A typical composite of a lake that could contain trout, bass, pike musky, panfish. Note that the three levels—high, medium and low—sometimes are in the same location in such a place as a dropoff beside a steep hill or cliff. These three bands show the upper layer of warmer water, the middle or median level and the lower, colder level. Below this in a deep lake, no fish will be found because the water temperature is too low, no light can bring forth an ecology to develop life for bait and gamefish.

Travel around this lake by studying the diagram and seek out the hot spots. Look for such areas in the lake to be fished and follow the temperature line for the season and fish species being sought.

with all kinds of conditions. The first—or shoreline—is the surface fishing level, the second line out would put the flies down to the ten-foot level. The last band is the area for deep trolling.

The fall of the year is a very good time to fish and it is almost as good as springtime. With the coming of colder nights, lowered sun angles and resultant lower averaging water temperatures, a surface cooling takes place. This acts the reverse of the spring turnover. With the surface water now again cooled to about 40 degrees, all of the lake's water is back at about the same temperature. Add fall winds to mix the water up a bit and fishing becomes great. The fish that have been sitting it out a few feet down in their cooler environment now feed and flip their tails on the surface to grab minute flies and bugs plus chasing the schools of minnows and other baitfish that are on their menu.

Then freezing temperatures come to the lake surface and the fish go down to the intermediate level. Now their surface action is over. The ice sets in and the fish go dormant. Once again it's time for the fisherman to go to the library for his reading and to the sporting goods shows for his therapy.

ARTIFICIAL IMPOUNDMENTS

Manmade lakes contain the same temperature and chemical problems as natural lakes. The only difference, basically, is that manmade lakes mature quickly and develop through the formative stages in a very few years. The same water turnover during the season takes place like clockwork. The shoreline develops its feed and harboring areas for all fish and insect life. Most impoundments are far deeper, however, than most natural lakes. This means that a lot of the impoundments' waters are barren of fish life. Way down deep, the water becomes too heavy and little light can develop the natural ecology to support baitfish, much less the bigger gamefish. So most of the deep impoundment is devoid of life and is like a desert. The most active areas, then, will be along the shore, the islands, reefs and extensions of the bottom which reach up near or to the surface.

Manmade lakes go through development stages where the fishing is fine for a few years following the initial plantings of fish and the maturing of the right ecological set-up to foster good gamefish development. With tremendous fish growth, fine catches of big fish are recorded, but with this extreme growth the fish can become stunted unless anglers take enough gamefish to keep the numbers reduced. Stunted fish result from fish overpopulation and a lack of food. If this condition persists, the fishing will fall off considerably and in some cases the gamefish will virtually disappear. In exceptional cases, stronger fish will gradually take over the lake. Brown trout, for example, will kill off brook trout. Pike and musky will all but eliminate panfish and even bass. With adequate study and positive action on the part of conservation departments in cooperation with the watershed authorities, an equitable gamefish population can be maintained to take care of anglers' needs and good ecological balance.

One of the serious problems with manmade lakes is their sometimes violent changes in level. When water is drained away from the lake at the wrong time, spawning fish are killed, much silt is washed into the lake and temperatures are varied by this water level to the point where ecological balance is impossible to maintain. Lessons are constantly being learned by management authorities with an eye to keeping such water impoundments producing good recreational fishing. An implicit objective is that the fishing be kept up to the quality of that to be found in natural lakes.

Learning to fish one of these impounded lakes must take into consideration the changing water levels, the period of the lake's maturity and the relative quality of the fishing—particularly the degree of balance being maintained in the various species of gamefish, natural food fish and others.

Again, local know-how is sometimes as important as scientific know-how and, if a little luck is mixed in, so much the better.

8

~~~~~~

The Fun of Fly Tying

IT IS TIME to start in on the basics of a great art, that of tying artificial flies with which to catch all manner of gamefish from panfish, trout and bass to the saltwater varieties. Along the way the fly tier will become part inventor, part artist craftsman, part entomologist and part an adherent to the traditions fostered by men and women everywhere who tie flies for their own enjoyment and some also who tie for their livelihood.

WHAT IT'S ALL ABOUT

Fly tying is a simple operation when taken step by step. The following pages show just that, as simply as possible, so that it can be discovered quickly just how easy it is and how much fun there is to it.

There is a particular thrill of anticipation as the mind's eye heralds the creation—no matter how humble at first, or imperfect —being gobbled up by a fish that has been fooled both by the artistry of its creation and its delivery to the water.

Fly tying has been called a Duke's mixture of practical fish lore and a smattering of biological study of live insects and food fish. The ingredients include varicolored feathers, a conglomeration of fur, tinsel, yarn, quills and wire, topped off with a generous amount of imagination and creative ability.

Like a good chef, the fly tier combines famous recipes with his own concoctions in hopes of making fishes' mouths water.

Since the days of Thaddeus Norris and Theodore Gordon, interest in American angling has zoomed from a veritable handful of anglers to an enthusiastic army of over thirty million. Quite naturally, fly tying, too, has progressed and grown accordingly.

The words "fly tying" round out the word "complete" when it comes to the enjoyment of angling. Not that it is impossible to derive heaps of satisfaction from fishing with "boughten" flies, but there is a great sense of achievement when you tie your own.

Years ago when only standard patterns were used, it was simpler for the trout to recognize and remember them! The art of fly tying was practiced by only a few and these men and women supplied practically all of the artificial flies and lures that were available. However, today's standard patterns have increased by leaps and bounds, not to mention patterns by Tom, Dick and Harry of our angling fraternity.

The angler who believes in the imitation school of tying, that is, forming a fly to directly imitate the real thing, has a clear and unlimited field of experimentation ahead of him; for certainly there is a lot of room for the perfection of natural nymph, wet fly and streamer patterns. Dry flies, too, can be developed for individual situations and requirements.

Fly tying in the off season offers many hours of interest and relaxation as well as an opportunity to apply the knowledge gained from days spent on the stream in the previous season. Certainly there is much to be learned from fellow tiers. Fly tying "on the spot", the selecting of an insect from the water and duplicating it right then and there, is an exciting experience, especially when the new creation catches a fish.

ABOUT TRADITIONAL PATTERNS

Many of the traditional patterns have quite a story. The Red Hackle, one of the most famous of all time, dates back to the period of Biblical history. The Beaverkill fly was tied first about 1850 by Harry Prichard, an American. He patterned it after an English fly and named it for his favorite stream, the Beaverkill in Sullivan County New York. The Bivisible family of flies, wingless all-hackle flies with a few rounds of white in the front, were originated by Edward R. Hewitt for use on the Neversink, another famous New York Catskill Mountain stream. The Gray or Leadwing Coachman was created by an Englishman, Henry R. Francis, around 1850, but Tom Bosworth, who was coachman to King George IV of England, William IV and Queen Victoria, was the originator of the Coachman fly.

The Quill Gordon was the product of the famed Theodore Gordon, tier of the first American dry flies. He tied for the well-remembered A. E. Hendrickson of Scarsdale, New York, for whom the Hendrickson pattern was named. The Parmacheene Belle was first tied by Henry P. Weels in 1878 and named after Parmacheene Lake in Maine. The fly was supposed to imitate the fin of a brook trout.

There are thousands of fly patterns, each bearing its own story. Many have become famous as fish getters for very good reasons. First because of publicity and fame of the tiers, and secondly, they have been used more consistently than many others. In today's age, when there are hundreds of thousands of tiers, there are bound to be locally tied favorites for particular times of the year on specific bodies of water.

WET AND DRY FLIES—CLOSELY RELATED

It is good, wherever one fishes, to pick up local patterns at the tackle stores and from outfitters and guides. Their patterns are not tied to catch fishermen, but to catch fish.

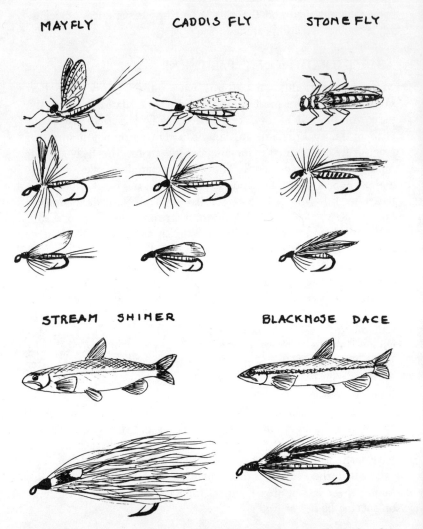

Figure 8-1. Shown here are the three basic staple insect foods found in trout streams that are imitated by dry and wet flies—the Mayfly, caddis fly and stone fly.

Below these are two very basic minnows upon which trout and other gamefish feed. The stream shiner imitated by the bucktail, for example, and the blacknosed dace imitated by the streamer fly.

It is suggested that the would-be tier learn first by selecting easy and uncomplicated patterns until he gets the "feel" of the equipment and until the steps become smooth and almost second nature. Do not start out by inventing your own flies. Follow the dressings of the experts. Then, study the insects and minnows and baitfish and try to simulate them. That is the time one's creativity will pay off.

To sum up—dry-fly, nymph and wet-fly fishing are closely related. While wet flies are basically designed to imitate nymphs among other things, the reason for the closer nymph imitation is that during a specific insect hatch the trout tend to become finicky and when feeding on one particular insect species they are most selective. To meet this situation the imitation must go beyond general "simulation" to the faithful reproduction of the nymph in size, shape, coloration and general overall "looks." The nymphal imitation is preferred during these times over the more general effect of the wet fly, particularly in the clear-water fishing for brown trout in Eastern waters. True, wet fly patterns do produce during these periods, too, but it will be discovered that when both a wet fly and a nymph imitation of a specific insect are fished together, the nymph usually wins out. The wet fly on the other hand is generally a far better producer when a hatch is not in progress or even expected, and then it is taken for insects drifting in the current, perhaps from a hatch that has progressed well upstream. That is why the wet fly is commonly used as a fish locator, when the angler is casting over all likely places without any special plan in mind other than "bumping into a trout."

The artificial nymph is deadly because it represents the underwater or nymphal stage of the stream-bred insects, the most constant and varied all-season food readily available to the trout.

Nymph fishing is most productive just before and during hatching periods because the trout feed on nymphs as they are nearing the surface to emerge into the air-borne phase of their existence. The sport rivals any other type of angling for it offers the trout the facsimile of what it wants right where it wants it.

Development of nymph imitations started to gain a foothold in this country about fifty years ago when anglers began taking an interest in imitating the living stream insects after the manner of

their British forebearers. Alert fly tiers and later the trade realized
the value of these early findings and at once a number of "nymph
imitations" appeared on the tackle counters. Though far from
accurate and with little known about their presentation, they were
a start in the right direction simply because they took fish.

It is very unfortunate that much of the angling literature, especially from the earlier British writers, has been taken as gospel
over here, for it has created much confusion. English fishing techniques, based as they are for their placid chalk streams, are inno-
cently swallowed even today in America where the fish and
streams are totally different. With all due respect to those thor-
ough British writers, and especially the late friend of mine, G. E.
M. Skues, we must eliminate theories, ideas and traditions from
abroad and learn the basics of our American fishing. A working,
practical knowledge based on natural laws has made fishing more
entertaining and productive thanks to the works of James Leisenring, Edward R. Hewitt, Ernie Schweibert, Pete Hidy, Ray Bergman, Preston Jennings, Art Flick, Jim Quick and many many others too numerous to mention. Their books are milestones in the
development of the scientific and practical approach to American
trout fishing and the art of fly tying to imitate natural trout foods,
and ways to fish them.

As is the case in exact imitation in dry flies, only a small
percentage of the thousands of insects found in or along the
stream are of serious consequence to the angler. To be able to
recognize these and know their habits is for all practical purposes
sufficient. With this knowledge, the angler can take just a few
minutes before the first cast or during a lull to examine the speci-
mens from the stream, or from the stomach of a trout, match the
artificial to them and then proceed with confidence that he is on
the right track.

FLY TYING MATERIALS

Materials for fly tying are unending in possibilities, but they do
break down into certain categories such as furs, wools, chenilles,
and various woven materials, feathers, tinsels, and hooks.

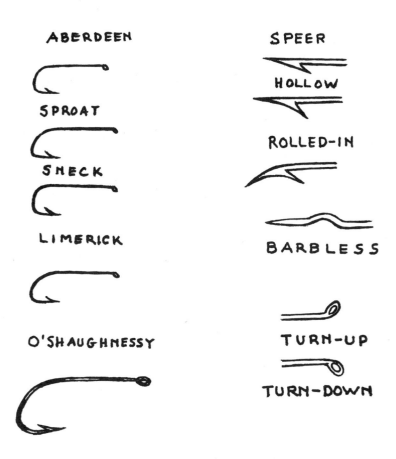

ABERDEEN

SPEER

HOLLOW

SPROAT

ROLLED-IN

SNECK

LIMERICK

BARBLESS

O'SHAUGHNESSY

TURN-UP

TURN-DOWN

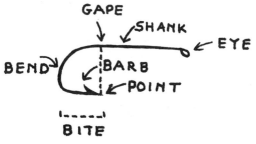

GAPE

SHANK

EYE

BEND

BARB

POINT

BITE

Figure 8-2.   Hook types.

Hooks

Sizes and styles vary. For first-learning, do not try to use hooks below size 10. Later it is possible to go to the smaller sizes. Hooks range in size from 24 (smallest) to 4's for the biggest flies. They also vary as to bend/curve, shank length and with either turn-up or turn-down eyes. A starting supply would include in Mustad Brand (100 hooks to a box) 94840, 3906, 9671, 38941, 79580. Buy these in 1× to 3× long. That's enough to start with.

Fur

These can be had from fly tying suppliers or from the local furrier in strips and pieces of discard; pieces of these would be useful: red fox, gray fox, beaver, muskrat, raccoon, bobcat, and seal. (Both natural and dyed.)

Rooster Neck Hackles

Bought from fly tying sources in complete necks: brown (red game), dark brown, furnace, grizzly, white, cream, light ginger, cree, and dyed black, blue gray, dark blue dun.

Saddle Hackle

The longer hackles on the back of the rooster. Brown, white, badger, furnace, dyed blue dun, black, grizzly.

Feathers

An endless assortment is usable. Amherst pheasant, golden pheasant, silver pheasant, ringneck pheasant, mandarin duck, (all skins). Maribou selection all colors dyed, peacock whole stem feather, Mallard duck side or flank feathers, breast, both wings; same for woodduck, teal. Turkey-wing quills, Goose wing-quills, turkey tail-feathers. Grouse feathers (tail).

Body Materials

Wool yarns in various colors and thicknesses (can be separated for fine work). Chenilles in all colors, shades and thicknesses.

Colored threads of all sizes and colors. Silver and gold tinsels, narrow, medium and wide, oval and woven.

This list is only a basic start. A visit to a fly tying shop, or a look at a catalog from one of the mail-order houses and suppliers will offer a wider assortment as it is called for in the patterns one wishes to tie.

FLY TYING SET-UP

The proper vise, hackle pliers, bobbin for the tying thread and a long sharp pin and a pair of short, narrow and very sharp scissors are the essentials for tying. A good light, preferably mounted overhead, shining directly on the work and not into the eyes, is correct. The vise should be mounted on the edge of the work table, a table, incidentally that will be large enough to allow spreading out materials and hooks. Materials should be boxed or enveloped and moth-proofing of some sort used. Tinsel and silks and other spooled materials can be kept in a box. Orderliness is important.

The list below is by no means complete, but is adequate for the tying of many standard flies. It is best to buy materials sparingly and in not too much variety at a time until the routines of tying have been established and more specific material demands identified.

Vise

Thompson "A" is a traditional choice of the pros.

Bobbin

Stainless steel tubular bobbin that holds tying thread spool.

Hackle Pliers

Spring-type stainless steel (two pair).

Thread

For tying the pre-waxed thread in black and brown, in sizes 3/0 to 6/0. Tiny flies require 7/0.

Finish

Clear nail polish in bottle with brush. Clear spar varnish. Black lacquer, brown lacquer.

FLY-TYING STEPS

The following routines of tying should be followed regardless of pattern or materials used. Establish the habits of consistency in tying. Once the basic steps are learned it is merely a matter of changing materials and learning how to apply them.

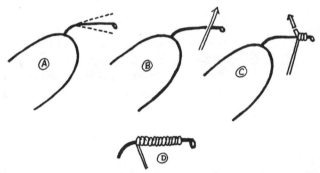

Figure 8-3. This is the method of placing the hook in the vise and attaching the line.

(A) Always level the hook, for winding will be easier when the hook is as level as possible. Hide the hook when possible, or hide as much of the point and barb as possible.

(B) Alway attach the line or begin a step TOWARDS the hook and in a down, up and over, down, under and back-toward-you direction. Do not tie in reverse direction.

(C) To secure line to hook, wrap over the line as shown and cut off surplus.

(D) Wrap the entire hook to a point just short of the bend of the hook. All work will be built on this wrapping. No material should be applied directly to the hook, else it will tend to slip.

Figure 8-4. Shown here are the steps for tying in the tail of the fly. Varied patterns call for many different kinds of materials, but they are all attached in the same fashion.

(A) Shows section of a golden pheasant crest feather having been cut from feather for tail material.

(B) This is placed between the fingers and laid firmly on the back portion of the hook. While placing it there, also grab the hook with the same fingers to secure the position of the feathers so that they will not flare out. Hold tight until the entire sequence of wrapping is finished.

(C) This is manner of wrapping on the material—line down and toward you—up, over, down and back under. (It is also advisable to slip the tying thread in between the fingers as you go up and around and slide the thread through the fingers so that it ties the material just where it is required on the hook.)

(D) Make one turn UNDER the material as shown and cut off the surplus.

(E) A short piece of wool yarn, shredded out for streamer pattern.

(F) Three hackle point tips, cut close to stem for nymph tails.

(G) Three strands of peacock tips for nymph or wet fly tails.

(H) Section of duck wing used for tail as per pattern demand.

(I) Short fur tail material and form of attachment.

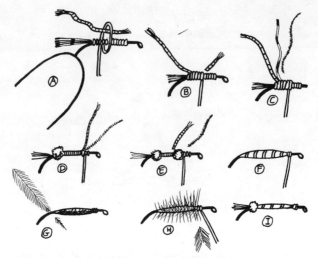

Figure 8-5.   Method of attaching body materials and forming bodies.

(A) With tail tied in and secured by half-hitch, a strip of simple wool yarn is used for practice, attached as shown and when secured . . .

(B) Surplus is cut off.

(C) Two or three different kinds of materials can be tied in, one at a time for future wrapping.

(D) Shows the egg sac of the Royal Coachman fly made of peacock herl and red yarn for body. The red yarn is wrapped over the strip of herl, since it will be used for the second sac.

(E) With the second sac tied in and secured, both surplus materials are cut off and the work secured by the half-hitch.

(F) Shows a typical bucktail or streamer (or wet fly) body tied with body material and gold or silver ribbing as called for in pattern.

(G) To Palmer-hackle a fly (or to make the woolyworm) tie in a hackle, point-first at base of body. This is wrapped on over the completed body either tightly, in Palmer-hackle style, or

(H)—Segmented with spaces in between the wrappings—the material surplus cut off and the work secured.

(I) Shows a typical wet fly or streamer with tail, sac, and ribbed body completed.

PRACTICE all these steps until they become second nature. Once learned it is only a matter of pattern requirements.

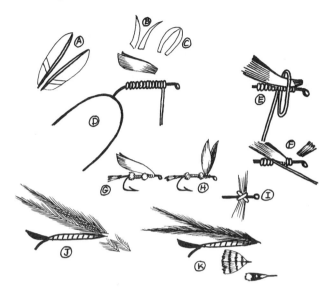

Figure 8-6. Method of tying in the wings.

(A) When a pattern calls for duck quill wings, a pair of duck primary feathers is selected—one from the left wing and one from the right wing. From these the wing sections are cut.

(B) For dry fly wings, the wings should fan out, so the sections are grasped in this manner. For wet fly wings, the sections are to fan IN toward each other and "married" (C).

(D) The wing section is then placed over the hook in the position shown. They are held tightly as was done in tying in the tail material—grasping the hook at the same time with the same fingers.

(E) Shows method of tying in the material. Remember to lead the thread in between the fingers as you wrap up, and over, and down again so that the thread ties in tightly for the downward pull. Make two rounds and run the third UNDER the wing material to set it firmly (F).

(G) Shows typical wet fly wing position secured.

(H) Shows typical dry fly wing position secured.

(I) To separate and secure dry fly wings, wrap the line in a figure eight as shown and secure with half-hitch.

(J) Wings for the streamer fly are tied in in the same fashion. (Bucktail, cut and selected for length and amount, is tied in in the same way, only more wraps will be required before cutting the surplus and securing.)

(K) Shows cheek feather and jungle cock feathers ready for tying in on each side of the hook.

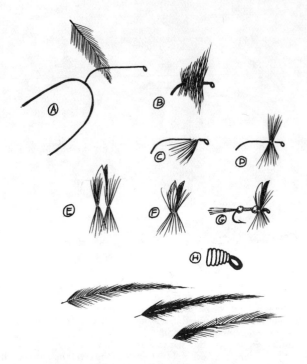

Figure 8-7. Hackling. Hackle for dry flies is selected with a minimum of WEB in the feather as shown at the bottom of the picture. Soft, webby hackle is selected for wet flies and streamers-bucktails.

(A) To tie an all-hackle fly—a good way to start learning—tie the hackle feather in by the tip at the bend of the hook. Wind the tying thread ahead to the tie-off point. Wrap the hackle in the same direction as you have been tying the thread—and keep the hackle tight—tie off, half-hitch and cut off surplus (B).

(C) Gather the hackle into the down position and wrap thread behind and around the bunch to make it conform to position.

(D) The dry fly position.

(E) Hackling in front of and behind the wings. On larger flies the hackle can be wound in figure eight style through the wings to separate and support the wings.

(F) Finished hackle and wings in traditional form.

(G) The finished fly.

(H) Tie off the head in an oval, smooth taper to the eye and whip finish. Then lacquer.

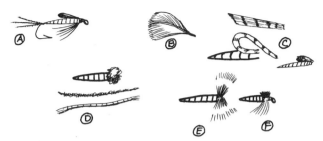

Figure 8-8. Tying the nymph. Tying the nymph involves the standard wet fly type body of fur, wool, combinations of fur-wool and ribbing of either quills, tinsel or different colored yarns or threads. The hackle should be sparse and set back or to the side as in tying the conventional wet fly. It can also be tied straight out, dry fly-style, with the upper and lower fibers cut off.

(A) Shows a typical wet-fly-type nymph with wing pad.

(B) A good wing pad is made from a selected covert feather from a duck wing. Select feathers with a slight curve from the wing shoulder. Strip off the fuzz and mount flat on the back of the nymph body.

(C) Wing pad made from feather fibers is tied in toward the back, circled forward again, drawn tight and tied off for a bunched-up form.

(D) A ball can be formed by wrapping peacock as is done in the Royal Coachman. A ball can also be made with yarn or even fur that can later be picked out for the fuzzy look. Another form of wing pad can be formed by dry fly hackling, cutting off the fibers on the back and trimming the remainder of the fibers to look like the conventional wet fly angle.

Much experimentation in nymph tying is in order, since there are few patterns or styles that have become traditional. (Your ideas are as good as anyone else's!)

Figure 8-9. The whip finish. This knot is preferred by many tiers as a secure knot to tie off the finished fly. The half-hitch is also considered enough to properly secure the fly, but unless it is tied in tight and the thread well waxed and then varnished, it can come apart.

To tie the whip finish, assemble as shown in the diagram and then revolve the loop (arrow) over the eye of the hook about three turns, loosely, and then allow the loops to tighten as you pull on the end of the line to draw it all tight. Cut off surplus in the behind position as shown.

VARIATIONS, SUBSTITUTES, ETC.

Now that the basic technique has been tried for streamer, bucktail, wet fly, nymph and dry fly based on conventional patterns and fly styles, it becomes apparent that tying should never vary to any extent from the basic principles except when an unusual effect is needed. Breaking the rules just for fun will gradually break down ability to tie really well. Shortcuts which do not in any way affect the durability and quality of the fly are acceptable, but be careful —this can lead to trouble.

Any variance from the norm must have a reason. And there are good reasons for a number of the flies known as variants.

In dry flies, variants are presently gaining in popularity. Many who start out to tie the Quill Gordon, for example, may find it difficult to locate a really good dun-gray hackle neck with stiff, shiny fibers. The best thing then is to substitute variant colors of hackle in a blend; for instance, a few turns of black and white Plymouth Rock, a smoky tan and dark tan or coal black. The end result may be even more alluring to the trout.

Further variance can be made in the proportions of the fly itself. To vary with legitimate reason, tie some of the same patterns on a hook one size smaller and use correspondingly less material. Remember that insects are somewhat transparent, unlike the heavily tied fly. The smaller the real insect the more transparent it seems.

What type of water will they be fished over? If it is a fast and bubbly mountain stream, use a fly that rides high on the water even if it will be constantly doused by bubbly waves and foam. If the fly is to be fished over more placid waters, it is better to have the fly sink down to the water level and ride in the surface film. Quite often the addition of a longer tail is necessary in order to have the fly ride correctly in the water, even though this would be contrary to conventional dimensions.

In the matter of dry fly wings, a substitute is often used for the duck quill sections. These are heavy and opaque while the insect's wings are light and transparent. Hackle feather tippets from the smallest feathers on the neck of the appropriate color may be used to great advantage. Long fibers of the right colored hackle can be substituted.

There are many dry fly patterns which call for fur bodies. Now, there is no real reason why they should be unless it is to help make the fly look more buggy. Most Mayfly insects have slim and glossy bodies, so actually, fur isn't the best way to show this to the fish. For instance, a gray hackle feather quill is sometimes substituted for a gray rabbit-fur body. If the Light Cahill pattern calls for a yellow-pink fox fur, a tan strip of turkey-tail feather fiber can be wrapped, or a striped hackle neck quill of light tan color can be used. There materials will not soak up as much water as the fur and will consequently be good for use on fast water. On the other hand, when fishing over the quieter waters of pools, the fur bodies can be the reason why the pattern takes fish.

Despite tradition many tiers are getting away from the use of wings, especially duck quill wings, preferring to make only a hackle fly with a middle section of darker hue hackle to represent the wings. Some tiers even use deer hair for the body hair, impala or even woodchuck hair which appears to the trout to imitate the veined wings of the Mayfly or stone fly wings.

From these few examples it can be seen where certain changes are definitely permissible when there is good reason or a lack of prescribed materials.

Many tiers are getting away from the fancy patterns of streamer flies except when they are tying them for stores who sell to the general public. Many expert fly tiers and well-known fishermen show one book of flies, but fish with another! Some of the best fishing flies would never sell!

The only part of fly tying in which there is virtually no rule is in tying the nymph. Since nymph fishing, especially in America, is a comparatively new angle in trout fishing, no traditions and hardly any patterns have become standards. Here then is the field for the experimenter! It is not easy to imitate the shiny and quick leg and gill motions of a nymph swimming through the water. The precise imitations of the hard body type may seem to us to be exact copies, but in the water they tend to look dead to the trout. It might be rightfully supposed that many so-called nymph imita-

Name	Head	Tail	Ribbing	Body	Hackle	Wing
PINK LADY	gray	ginger hackle barbules	gold tinsel	pink floss	ginger	light gray mallard quill
Brown BI-VISIBLE (black, gray)	black	brown hackle points			large badger fronted with white	
ROYAL COACHMAN	black	golden pheasant		(body; two peacock herls with red center between)	dark brown	white
LEADWING COACHMAN	black	brown hackle		peacock herl (thick)	brown	lead mallard
PARMA-CHEENE BELLE	black	red over white duck	gold	yellow floss	red & white	red over white duck
PROFESSOR	black	red duck	gold	yellow floss	brown	gray mallard breast
DARK CAHILL	black	brown hackle		gray wool	brown	woodduck flank feather
McGINTY	black	red feather over mallard flank	black chenille	yellow chenille	brown	white tipped mallard
BEAVERKILL and female Beaverkill	black	brown hackle		gray fur or wool (fem yellow yarn egg sac)	brown	gray mallard quill

	tail (color)	hackle barbules (color)		fur or wool (color) or dyed striped hackle quill	stiff hackle (color)	mallard dyed (color)
QUILL SERIES gray, olive, red	tan, black					
ADAMS	black	mixed barred Plymouth Rock and brown		gray fur or wool	mixed barred Plymouth Rock and brown	barred Plymouth Rock hackle points
QUILL GORDON	black	rusty blue dun or gray hackle barbules		striped peacock quill	blue or rusty dun or gray hackle	wood duck
MARCH BROWN	black	brown or furnace hackle barbules	gold tinsel	yellow fur or wool gold ribbed	brown	bronze mallard or woodduck flank
GOLD-RIBBED HARE'S EAR	black	cochy-blonde hue or brown hackle fibers	gold tinsel	gray fur or wool	cochy-blonde hue	gray mallard quill
PINK LADY (BRITISH)	gray	ginger hackle barbules	gold tinsel	pink floss	ginger	light gray mallard quill
LIGHT HENDRICKSON	black	blue dun hackle barbules		grayish cream fur or wool	blue dun	woodduck
BLACK GNAT	black	black hackle barbules		black fur or wool	black	dark gray mallard quill
LIGHT CAHILL	cream	light ginger hackle barbules		light cream fur or wool	light ginger	woodduck
GRAY WULFF	black	brown deer hair		gray fur or wool	blue dun	brown deer hair

Name	Head (color)	Tail (color)	Ribbing	Body (color) wool	Hackle (color)	Wing
BI-VISIBLES	brown, black					none

NYMPHS   Effective nymphs follow the general wet and dry fly body patterns with a contrived silhouette bump on the top of the shank just behind the eye. These are made from single small mallard wing covert feathers, folded over strips of mallard or woodduck flank feathers or even wound on peacock herl between the head and underhackle of the fly.

Name	Head	Tail	Ribbing	Body	Hackle	Wing or Pad
DARK HEN-DRICKSON	black	brown moose-mane	none	moosemane over built-up body	dark brown	dark covert feather
GREEN CADDIS	black			green floss	gray	gray snipped mallard
GREEN DRAKE	brown	lt. gray hackle points		cream fur or wool	cream	small cream covert or gray mallard
GRAY FOX	lt. gray	gray partridge	gold	rabbit	brown partridge	lt. gray
STONEFLY	black	two gold-brown hackle points	flat gold	brown floss	brown and yellow	dark turkey

Steelhead Flies	Head	Tail	Ribbing	Body	Hackle	Wing
CALIFORNIA	black	gold pheasant tippets		peacock herls yellow floss center	yellow	white duck quill

Fly Pattern Dressings	Head	Tail	Ribbing	Body	Shoulder	Wing
QUEEN BESS	black	gray squirrel		silver tinsel		yellow hair topped with gray squirrel
UMPQUA SPECIAL	red		thin gold	red floss gold back body	red	white hair red feather side strips
ALASKA MARY ANN	black	red fibers	silver flat tinsel	white floss		white Polar bear and jungle cock
SKYKOMISH SUNRISE	white	yellow and red hackle barbules	flat silver	red floss	red	white hair or Polar bear
Fly Pattern Dressings	*Head*	*Tail*	*Ribbing*	*Body*	*Shoulder*	*Wing*
BLACK GHOST	black	yellow hackle fibers	flat silver tinsel	tapered; black floss	yellow hackle throat; jungle cock eye	two white saddle hackles
GREEN GHOST	black		flat silver tinsel	orange floss	silver pheasant body feather jungle cock eye, peacock herl and white bucktail throat	four gray or pale green saddle hackles
GRAY GHOST	black		flat silver tinsel	orange floss	silver pheasant peacock herl white bucktail and gold pheasant crest throat; jungle cock eye	four gray saddle hackles

Fly Pattern Dressings	Head	Tail	Ribbing	Body	Shoulder	Wing
LIGHT EDSON TIGER	yellow	silver pheasant		peacock herl	red feather with jungle cock	yellow bucktail
DARK EDSON TIGER	black	yellow hair or golden pheasant crest		yellow chenille	red hackle or feather throat	light brown bucktail with jungle cock
SQUIRREL TAIL	black with yellow-black painted eye		oval silver tinsel	silver tinsel		white, topped with gray squirreltail hair
BLACK-NOSE DACE	black with yellow-black painted eye		oval silver tinsel	silver tinsel		white, black, brown bucktail
MICKEY FINN	black with yellow-black painted eye		oval silver tinsel	silver tinsel		yellow, red, yellow bucktail

Notes: For streamer-bucktails, bucktail hair is added to fly before cheek or jungle cock is tied in. For bucktail-streamers, the streamer feathers are added to the side of the bucktail before jungle cock or cheek is tied in.

Some tiers extend the feathers about a third of the way beyond the hook. To avoid the chances of fish striking too short, other tiers keep the material limited to the length of the hook and dress the fly more sparsely.

tions look like so much trash to a trout as he goes about his search trying to pick out live insects in the stream's flotsam.

Other anglers will love to pillage your fly supply and also ask you to tie flies for them. Allow this up to a certain point; that is, until you feel that they are definitely taking advantage of you. Beyond a certain point they will not appreciate your art, and your craft and skill will be wasted on them.

Trade? Yes! Give away? Sometimes. But better to teach them how to tie!

INDIVIDUAL FLIES—DESCRIPTIONS AND MATERIALS USED

It becomes very difficult to single out a handful of successful and widely used nymph patterns from the thousands tied by American tiers. As to conventional wet flies, the wet counterpart of the dry flies constitute a good selection. The steelhead flies are, by contrast, well respected "standards." See pages 136 through 141 for some well-known freshwater patterns.

SALTWATER FLIES

In tying saltwater flies, the sky is the limit in pattern design. This sport, being so relatively new (since the 1940's), has produced few so-called "standard flies" for any given species. True, individual fly tiers have developed killing patterns for specific gamefish, and for all saltwater gamefish for that matter, but it is still an art in its infancy, affording creative latitude for future development.

Basically the saltwater fly is the imitation of shrimp, minnows, school baitfish and in some cases worms that float on or near the surface. These should be tied on hooks that will self-destruct through rusting; stainless steel hooks should not be used. If a fish is too small or is to be released, the leader is cut above the fly. The hook soon rusts out due to the fish's saliva and saltwater corrosion.

Heavyweight, long-shank hooks of appropriate sizes are tied as is or weighted for sinking. Most saltwater anglers use the new sinking lines and short leaders, sometimes with a very short stainless steel leader to avoid the sharp teeth of the fish.

The patterns shown here are simple and general and are meant only as a guide. They'll catch fish when properly presented at the right time, but much experimentation is in order for specific fish under special conditions.

In tying saltwater flies, follow the directions for the tying of streamer and bucktail flies.

Figure 8-10.   Saltwater flies have not become standardized to any degree. Most of them are designed by local anglers for specific conditions and particular gamefish. The seven choices here show a selection that would suffice almost anywhere.

(1) *Ballyhoo* used for various Florida species.
    Hook: No. 1/0.
    Tail: Twelve white saddle hackles 4 inches long with two 1/32-inch mylar strips on each side.
    Body: Built-up with tying thread, painted green on top and white underneath. (Designed by Lefty Kreh, Miami, Fla.)

(2) *Frank Streamer* used for striped bass.
    Hook: No. 2/0.
    Tail: Frosty squirrel extending from body tubing.
    Body: Silver mylar tubing one inch longer than hook.
    Wings: Purple over white bucktail with heavy peacock herl topping, three inches long.
    Shoulders: Jungle cock eye feathers.
    Throat: Red hackle fibers.
    Head: Black. (Frank Lawrence, El Sobrante, Calif.)

(3) *Galli-Nipper* used for striped bass and others.
    Hook: No. 1/0, 3 XL shank.
    Tail: Red wool ¼ inch long.
    Body: Silver mylar piping, wrapped.
    Wings: Yellow bucktail, 3½ inch long.
    Cheeks: 2½ inches long, grizzly hackles, placed high on each side.
    Throat: Red wool ¼ inch long.
    Head: Gold. (J. Edson Leonard, Barrington, Rhode Island)

(4) *McNally Smelt*, various species.
    Hook: No. 3/0.
    Body: Silver mylar tinsel.
    Wings: Heavy white bucktail 4½ to 5 inches long, fifteen to twenty peacock herl strands of same length over.
    Cheek: Mallard breast feather. (Tom McNally, Chicago, Ill.)

(5) *Bluefish Streamer*.
    Hook: No. 2/0, 4XL.
    Body: Rear quarter wrapped with fine diameter red mylar piping.
    Wing: Yellow bucktail 1 inch long, ahead of short body. (C. Boyd Pfeiffer, Baltimore, Maryland)

(6) *Menhaden Streamer* for striped bass and bluefish.
    Hook: Nos. 1/0-3/0.
    Body: None.
    Wings: Bucktail, 3½ inches long, white underneath, pink above hook, blue on top, all tied forward and then back around hook and secured with a red collar of thread ½ inch behind hook eye.
    Eye: Painted orange with black center on pink stripe between collar and hook eye. (Morton Ross, Massapequa Park, Long Island, N.Y.)

(7) *Bub's Sand Eel*, striped bass.
    Hooks: No. 1/0 (two).
    Thread: Red.
    Body: Hooks in tandem using 30-pound leader material, 4-inch mylar tubing covering with forward hook point through tubing.
    Tail: ¼ inch mylar strands unraveled from tubing.
    Wing: Two 4-inch badger saddle hackles tied down at tail.
    Throat: Eight long peacock sword strands. (Bub Church, Plainfield, N.J.)

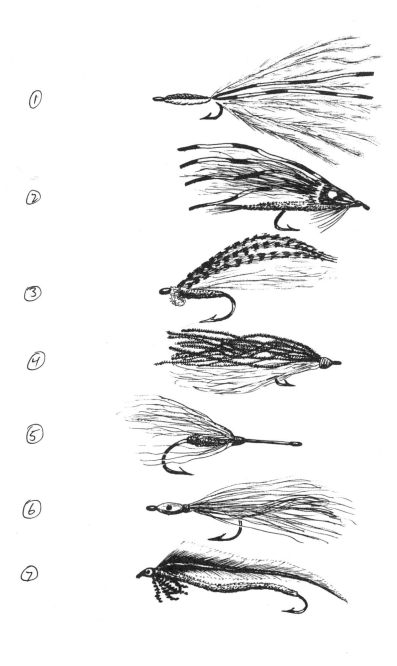

9

Popular Game Fish

THE BROWN TROUT, an import from Europe in 1880, long ago became completely at home in the United States and is accepted as a native. It is the most finicky, selective and hard-to-catch trout of our classic streams. Able to thrive in waters where the brook trout would not survive and where the rainbow would not be comfortable, the brown grows to prodigious size and as it grows its feeding becomes highly selective. It is thus the fly fisherman's favorite and most difficult fish to entice.

Broad rivers with long slicks and runs, deep pools and broken water harbor them. Even the stocked browns seem to adapt quickly to natural feeding on aquatic insects and land-bred flies. The angler who has been brought up on fishing for brown trout will generally find all other species comparatively easy to catch, including the much touted steelhead and the Atlantic salmon.

Beginners, following instructions and guidance from old hands or knowledgeable guides can catch Atlantic salmon far easier than can an angler turned loose to catch a trout on the Beaverkill in the New York Catskills, for example. The brown trout angler usually becomes a fly tier since the fish he seeks seems to warrant extra talent in fly design as well as presentation on the stream.

Nymphs, wet flies, streamers, bucktails, and tiny midges are used for them. Because of their extremely finicky nature, long, thin leaders are required and good casting ability and knowledge of where to cast are additional requirements.

Their fight is a combination of the brook trout's body roll and the rainbow's run. While they are not noted for their spectacular jumping ability, they will take to the air much more frequently than the brook trout.

When living in clear cool rivers, their colors are exceptional, almost rivaling the brook trout and the golden trout for beauty.

BROOK TROUT

The famed Eastern brook trout, *Salvalinus Fontanalis*, is not a trout but a char, similar in species to the lake trout and the Dolly Varden.

The native waters of the brook trout were once limited to the streams and lakes of the Northeast, from the Appalachian Mountains to as far south as Georgia. Today with the extensive stocking programs of both states and private individuals, the brook trout has grown to large size in the Rocky Mountain West and even in streams of the Far West—California, in particular.

The brook trout requires clearer, cooler water, more sheltered tree-lined and rocky streams. It is a fish of the deep shaded holes, not a fish like the brown trout that will survive in open streams. Nor will the brooky reside in typical rainbow water with its fast unbroken stretches of white water. Nor is the brook trout a subtle fish. It is far easier to catch, particularly on flies than the other species. Given a stream where all three trout have been stocked, the brook trout will usually be the first to be fished out.

But the brook trout makes up for these unfavorable comparisons by its indescribable beauty, its particular body roll fight, as opposed to the long runs and sensational jumps attributed to the rainbow.

It is not as good a fish for the dry fly and will be found less prone to take the dry fly if the simple drift and skitter wet fly fisherman is in the competition.

Brookies are attracted to the more colorful flies, particularly streamers and big wet flies. They will take the big dry flies, such as the Royal Coachman and other fanwings over the more subtle dingy and sparse, small dry flies.

LANDLOCKED SALMON

First cousin to the Atlantic, the smaller, though just-as gamey landlocked salmon is a prize given only to those anglers visiting the Northeastern sector of the country in the same waters and lakes in which the native brook trout abound. The landlocked salmon does not migrate to the sea, but resides in deep cold lakes, spawning in the tributary streams of these lakes. Best time to fish for landlocks is in the spring after the ice has left the lakes. Then the salmon are feeding largely at the surface on insects, but mainly on the smelt and cisco herring that school at that time. Later in the season they descend to a comfortable temperature deep in the lakes and trolling is then the only way to get them unless they are seen rising to a specific hatch of flies.

Flies of a specific type—the tandem, two-hook streamer flies are cast and trolled on or near the surface at the point of an inlet to a lake, along deep drop-offs and in and along the connecting steams between lakes.

Landlocks are much smaller than Atlantic, averaging a pound or two with three, five and six pounders the exception.

While they can be caught on bait, most anglers fish for them with spinning lures, but the streamer fly and on occasion, the dry fly offer the epitome of sport here.

For action, the landlock is unrivaled for his weight, making no comparison with the rainbow trout or smallmouth bass. It is a fish that once caught will set a precedent in the annals of personal thrills.

With a range that is limited and artificial stocking unproductive, the landlock is holding to its home grounds despite warming lake temperatures and fishing pressure. Like the golden trout it can be considered an endangered species.

RAINBOW TROUT

Salmo gairdneri, the rainbow trout once only native to the West Coast of America from Alaska to Southern California, is now native to almost all streams and lakes that can sustain any kind of trout population. In its steelhead form, that of the andronomous ascender of streams when in season to spawn, it is limited to Pacific coastal rivers and streams. It is a family of many sub-species such as the Kamloops, Nelson redsides, Kern River, Shasta and San Gorgonio, with the California golden trout the most exotic and beautiful of the strains. The rainbow as a migratory steelhead is more silver in color with a faint pink stripe down its lateral line. As the fish remains in fresh water its colors deepen and the black spots begin to appear.

Due to its extreme north-south range and the varied conditions of the lands surrounding the waters in which it lives, the rainbow shows variances of color and shape from bright silver with only faint gray or green backs, mild pink stripe and few indistinct spots, to dark green-olive-blue backs, orange and pink striping leading to almost blood red on the gill covers and dramatic and closely spaced spots the whole length, from tips of tail to nose. In shape, the rainbow can be extremely slim with a small head, to fat and bulky with large head and strong jaws. Its colors generally become more intense during the spring migration for spawning. Those fish in the clear lakes can grow to weights of almost forty pounds. The migratory steelhead reaches this poundage, but generally runs to only ten or twenty as a rule. The rainbow of the streams range from half a pound to ten or fifteen, depending on the size of the stream and the amount of supporting food.

Its spawning habits are similar to the Atlantic salmon.

Transplants of the rainbow eggs and fry taken from a specific stream and planted sometimes thousands of miles away will eventually return to their native waters as shown by tagging.

As an example of the variation that can take place in characteristics and color, note that the golden trout, the most beautiful distinctive rainbow trout of the High Sierras of California living at an altitude of 10,000 feet would seem to be a separate species, but if the eggs are raised at a hatchery at a much lower altitude, the fish revert back to the normal rainbow. The only way that the golden trout will remain distinctive through stocking is to maintain the strain at its normal altitude and guard against changes.

Due to the smaller lakes and streams in which it is found, the golden rarely reaches a weight of over a few pounds, and generally, in the mountain creeks runs to only a pound or less. The markings are dramatic and rival the brook trout in beauty.

Like the Atlantic salmon, the rainbow is also known as a leaper, for it is far and away the most active trout in America, leaping and jumping high into the air when hooked or when actively feeding on surface-floating flies or flies that are buzzing about just above the water surface. When hooked underwater, the rainbow generally streaks out in long fast rushes rather than body roll or twist as do the brook and brown trout. If there is room to do so, rainbow of, say, three pounds will likely run out fifty yards of line backing before it is tired and will jump many times as it is brought into the net.

As with the other trout species, the rainbow feeds mainly on aquatic insects, crustations and shrimp, minnows and trout fry and—when present—frogs and other aquatic or semi-aquatic creatures. The steelhead's first order of food are the salmon eggs that drift down to it from above where the salmon are spawning. If the steelhead or rainbow are present in the stream when there is not a salmon spawning in progress, they will still take the eggs or fly imitations that resemble them. This is why colors such as red and orange are present in many typical steelhead flies.

The rainbow trout, particularly in the East, has found basically good water in the streams that lead into impoundments and reservoirs. In the summer the fish can go deep into the lakes and migrate into the feeder streams to spawn. In one stream of this type, one planting of rainbows 40 years ago was sufficient to establish a permanent fishery producing two to five-pound rainbows, whereas in the same waters, even the brown and brook trout must be continually restocked. While they will not tolerate the warmer temperatures equitable to the brown, the rainbow fares much better than the brook trout in planted streams. The brook trout has retired to the highest and coolest tributaries of streams, even into mere trickles, and the larger fish drop down to waters below in small numbers. The rainbow, however, takes the entire stream and lake system into account and seems to thrive well even in semi-polluted water. In this respect he does much better than the brook trout.

As to fishing technique, the rainbow is caught on all methods and styles of flies, from trolled streamers to deep-fished wet flies, weighted nymphs and floating dry flies that imitate stream minnows, aquatic and land-bred insects. In most good American streams, all three species of trout are available and rainbows are caught in the same ways as the others. The rainbow exhibits a much greater preference for the faster stretches of streams and the deeper fast currents than do the brook and brown trout.

CUTTHROAT TROUT

The cutthroat trout, *salmo clarki*, is also called Snake River cutthroat, Yellowstone cutthroat, Montana black spotted trout, Tahoe trout, Colorado trout, intermountain and coastal cutthroat. It is very similar to the basic rainbow in breeding, migration and feeding habits.

The cutthroats that live on the Eastern slopes of the Rocky Mountains and in areas where there is no access to the Pacific cannot ascend saltwater rivers to spawn. Those that are so "land-locked" therefore live in ways similar to the rainbow.

The coloration of the two varieties are quite different, the Inland variety have an orange, yellow cast with olive backs, rarely exhibiting the pink lateral stripe such as found on the rainbow. The sea run variety are more bluish-green. Both are generously spotted with more and smaller spots than the rainbow.

The main identification mark is the red slit under both lower jaw bones that is quite predominant. The reddish cast sometimes is found also on the gill covers.

While judged to be not quite as hefty a fighter as the rainbow, the cutthroat does offer quite a sporting battle, reaching the size of forty pounds in the extreme with 10 and 15-pound fish more common. It thrives in lakes, rivers and even tiny creeks high up in the mountains or in low valleys close to sea level.

Standard trouting techniques take cutthroats readily, for this fish is not as selective as the brown or brook trout. It has not been stocked in waters beyond its natural range for fishery experts still prefer the rainbow.

The cutthroat reaches its heaviest weight and greatest abundance in British Columbia. It is still found in Wyoming because of artificial propogation. It was once the only trout found in that state.

ARCTIC GRAYLING

This is a fish primarily of Alaskan and Canadian waters, although found in a few rivers and streams of Montana, Idaho, Wyoming and Utah where they have been successfully planted with natural reproduction improving in these waters through extensive stocking developments. The Michigan Grayling was once prevalent in that state but the last of these fish, while being held in the Menomonie Hatchery, were devoured one Sunday afternoon in the 1930's by sea gulls.

The technical name of *thymallus arcticus* heads the family of grayling, there being mainly four strains such as the Baikal, Kamchatka and Montana and Michigan. The large sail-like dorsal fin differentiates this fish from other salmonoids. Their color differs widely, even within small geographic distances, varying from a deep purple to rose and even gold to a clear white silver. The fins are generally a dusky yellowish green or gray.

They feed on insects and dry and wet flies and offer top sport when they are on the food or active to a rise. They spawn March to June, depending on the temperatures and location and in streams that enter the lakes as feeders. They run from 15 pounds in the extreme to fish of two to four pounds, the more regular fare.

The grayling has a very small mouth for its size, but not necessarily a soft mouth, so flies or at least hooks of small size are recommended. Unlike the trout, grayling run in schools and when a school is located almost every cast will get a rise. They are not as easy to hook as other trout, but their rise to the fly is dramatic and their body-rolls when on the hook are impressive.

They are very leader-shy so downstream fishing with slack line is usually the most effective fishing method. Standard trout fly patterns are popular. The western provinces of Canada between Alaska and the United States contain hundreds of rivers and lakes where grayling fishing is tops.

DOLLY VARDEN TROUT

Salvelinus malma, the Dolly Varden trout of the West is a char of the brook trout family, its color varying from clear silver to a well spotted pattern over a dark red and orange background. Shaped like a brook trout it also exhibits faint vermiculation marks on the upper back and top sides to the lateral line, similar to the brook trout.

The main variation between the two species is the size of the Dolly, a twenty to forty-pound fish as a rule. It thrives in cold mountain streams and the deep lakes of Montana, Idaho, Colorado and up into Canada and southern Alaska. On the West Coast it is found in northern California streams and lakes, in eastern Oregon and Washington.

It spawns in the fall as does the brook and brown trout and, when possible, migrates to the sea along the same pattern as the steelhead.

Its feed is aquatic insects, land-bred blow-ins and basic minnow and fry population of the stream or lake. It can be most destructive when it grows to large size, often depleting the brook and brown trout population, not to mention forage and baitfish in the same water.

It is welcomed because of its size and taste by most anglers, but the Dolly plantings in some waters have brought despair because of its extensive predation.

It is a gamey fish, fighting in typical brook trout fashion with body roll and twist, and with only occasional long runs. It is relatively poor on the dry fly and its death knell is the wet fly fished deep.

HYBRID TROUT

Fish culturists have been experimenting with trout hybrids since 1877 in the United States, first at the Caledonia Hatchery at Mumford, New York. Many new species have been developed in order to create strains of trout that would better suit the warming waters of less remote streams and lakes. Objectives were also to create gamier fish for more sport.

The *splake* has been developed from the brook and lake trout (both chars) and has done fairly well, though it is difficult to reproduce naturally.

The *tiger trout* is the cross between the female brown and the male brook trout. Trouble still persists in its development for natural hybrid production. It is a good fish, good fighter and acclimates well.

The *cutbow trout* is a cross between the cutthroat and the legitimate rainbow (an occurrence that often happens naturally in the West). This fish has been partially successful in programs toward its natural reproduction.

The *trousal* is a cross between the brown and the Atlantic salmon and has not done too well.

The *brownbow* is a brown trout female crossed with a male rainbow and is a pretty fish, but, again, much has to be accomplished before it is a natural spawner.

Actually the transplanting of the brook trout to the West and the rainbow to the East with the brown coming in from Europe has been a godsend to American trout fishing, and most anglers feel that more projects in this direction are of more importance to them than concentrating on the development of hybrids.

Distribution of hybrids is on such a minor scale it is not worth recounting. Future years will provide records on the development of hybrids into natural spawners and how they rate in stamina against other species and the changing environment.

AMERICAN SHAD

The American shad (*alosa sapidissima*) is found on both coasts of the United States, ascending the rivers to spawn in the manner of the Atlantic salmon. The hickory shad is another species of shad of interest to anglers, though lacking in size, fighting ability and taste.

American shad are found mostly along the entire Atlantic Coast as far south as Florida. In Florida, the St. Johns River has a spring run of big fish ranging from 2 to 6 pounds. The hickory is found in the more southerly states, remaining below the Gulf of Maine.

The hickory shad has a longer projecting lower jaw. It runs from 1 to 3 pounds, maximum 6 pounds, while the American will sometimes weigh 8.

While the sport of shad fishing extends to the Gulf of St. Lawrence, the biggest runs are in the lower New England states and Virginia with the Connecticut River through that state and Massachusetts being the most famous. Pollution control on many New England rivers has seen the return of the shad and in some cases the migration of the sea-run brook trout as well. At one time these rivers also attracted Atlantic salmon, as did the great Hudson River and its big system. Chesapeake Bay and rivers of that region also have big runs of shad.

Originally found only on the East Coast, the shad is now found in rivers of northern California with Oregon and Washington having their steady runs in such fine salmon and steelhead rivers as the Umpqua, Coos and, or course, the magnificent Columbia.

The shad of the more northern rivers spawn only once, in the manner of the Pacific salmon, and die after that spawn while the fish of southern waters may spawn twice or more depending on the conditions.

The meat of the shad is known round the world as a first-class table fish with shad roe savored as a specialty of the house. While shad are commercially netted in the brackish waters of bays and harbors this has not depleted the numbers of fish available to sportsmen.

Fly fishing is the ideal method for shad and some flies are especially tied for them. They are either trolled or cast in fishing the holding pools and runs. Light tackle is preferred despite the terrific fighting ability of these fish. A rod with a soft tip is especially recommended since the mouth of the shad is very soft and almost herring-like, making the snapping strike almost impossible to perform. If the fish is held too severely, the hook will surely pull out of the soft flesh. On the other hand, if the fish is allowed to fight too long, the hook will tear out from excessive wear. Shad flies are weighted and fished from a foot to three feet down. The head of the fly is usually beaded with a red or yellow bead. The fly body is generally silver tinsel and the hackles or wings of short bright colors. Sparsely dressed trout streamers and bucktails usually produce as well.

BASS

Largemouth bass (*micropterus salmoides*) is probably the most popular and important sport freshwater fish in the United States and parts of southern Canada. It is also known as the green bass, green trout, Oswego bass and black bass. It is distinguished from its cousin, the smallmouth, by its jaw which extends far back from the eye and its mouth, larger than that of the smallmouth. There is generally a greenish or dark colored lateral line of indistinct markings throughout its length, while the smallmouth has vertical marking bars similar to those found on the muskellunge.

The bigmouth was once limited to the area of southeastern Canada through the Great Lakes and down the Atlantic Coast as far south as Maryland. (The Florida bass of gigantic size is a subspecies from the purely technical standpoint.) Now, through successful introduction, the largemouth is found in Southern California, the Rocky Mountain states, Oregon and Washington.

Actually the range of the largemouth overlaps the more northern areas generally inhabited by the smallmouth and lakes and rivers often contain both species, both being caught by the same methods and on the same lures and flies. Actually there is little difference in fishing for them with large Wulff-type dry flies, bass bugs, streamers or bucktails. Large wet flies, either trolled or cast, will also take either species in lakes, rivers and streams. The table qualities of both are about the same and rated excellent, though there are some who prefer the smallmouth from the colder waters of northern rivers.

As to the fighting qualities of the two, the smallmouth seems to have more bulldoggedness and fights harder and longer than the largemouth, but again this is a matter of conditions. Any contest between catching a smallmouth in warmer waters against a largemouth in colder waters would be hard to judge, the smallmouth is generally a more northern fish with a preference for colder water than suits the largemouth. Some believe this makes him a more vigorous fighter. The largemouth, however, is generally heavier and breaks water perhaps more often than the smallmouth when trying to throw a lure and this, no doubt, enhances his popularity with fishermen.

The smallmouth (*micropterus dolomieui*) is a prime river fish in the states of Oregon and Washington and in the rivers of the New England states plus Pennsylvania and Michigan. Maine and New Brunswick have about the finest smallmouth bass fishing in America and there bass have taken over many waters where formerly the brook trout and landlocked salmon were once the prime attractions.

Both species spawn in the late spring, building nests in the clear and shallow sections of a lake or in the current-swept elbows of rivers and streams. They guard their nests savagely, but in the states that allow fishing for them during the spawning season, they are comparatively easy to take then on floating bugs and flies cast over the nests. Later in the season the bass tend to hide in heavy weed growth and the deeper section of lakes, coming to the surface only when attracted by insects, minnow schools and other food. Night fishing with bugs and large flies is effective when the weather is hot and the lake water warm. Essentially a warmer water fish that the trout, the bass, particularly the largemouth, will inhabit the shallower portions of the lake while the smallmouth will go down deeper, hiding out in the rockier sections of the lake or river.

The largemouth reaches its greatest size in Florida (and now California) testing in at from ten to fifteen pounds, while the smallmouth will at best attain a weight of from four to six pounds —possibly eight pounds in the extreme.

Since the advent of large reservoirs and impoundments in many states both bass have become standard big game fare and have greatly contributed to the growth of fishing as a national sport throughout the U.S.A. and southern Canada. Add to this, the increase in farm ponds in which bass fishing has been expanded and this, too, has further developed the nation's fishing sport.

There is also much private water, some owned by clubs, and these waters, too, are heavily stocked and heavily fished, for if a lake is allowed to grow too many bass they become stunted and are less prized. Hence big bass are found generally where there is the most fishing, a situation which differs markedly from the conditions needed for growing big trout.

The same lakes that contain bass also contain a great grouping of species categorized as panfish. In big impoundments and large lakes bass compete for food and popularity with pike and muskellunge as well, so the sport in this type of water is varied and exciting.

Perhaps the most subtle form of fishing is for the smallmouth found in the lower reaches of famous trout streams. These bass are taken on dry flies, nymphs and streamers fished in the same way as used for trout. In fact, while trout fishing, big bass will sometimes be hooked and even when the angler is searching for a big bass, big trout may take his bass offering with utter abandon.

Trolling for bass, particularly the smallmouth in northern lakes, employs the tandem-hooked streamer similar to that family of flies as used for landlocked salmon and lake trout. Two of three large and gaudy wet flies dragged and flipped on the surface of a calm lake near the shallows also produce, particularly in the early morning and evening when the lake surface is calm and glassy.

As more and more streams and rivers are dammed for flood

control, power and water supply, the lakes so made will become excellent bass fishing locations, so bass are assured a permanent and growing future in American angling sport.

PANFISH

This big class of fish from the fly fishing point of view can be treated together not because of their minor importance, but because they form the major angling available especially for beginners and youngsters.

Panfish are found wherever there are lakes, backwaters, ponds, lazy rivers, slow streams and even swamps. They are all eager fly takers, especially the wet flies and a great deal of them will also take dry flies, being not at all finicky about either patterns or fault-free delivery. Often a school of fish can be located from which fish after fish can be taken in quick succession. Ultra-light gear is recommended, even finer than that of most light trout outfits. Small-size flies are needed because of the small mouths in this category. Often, too, a fish will suck in a dry fly several times before it is hooked, offering the beginner as well as the expert a great deal of fun.

In recent years farm ponds have increased, augmenting local panfish populations and lessening angling pressures on natural waters. The art of panfishing has it subtleties and panfish fly tiers are as avid about developing *taking* lures and flies as are trout fisherman. Most of the panfish species are found in company with both trout and bass. They are often taken unwillingly, perhaps, on small flies by the trout fisherman. Many high quality trout streams carry two or more species of these fish thus offering much variety.

In most lakes, panfish inhabit the shallower portions, seldom going lower than twenty feet and staying where lush weed growth offers protection from the bigger fish and furnishing insects and small minnows for their needs.

Most spawn in the spring in company with the bass along the lake shores. They range in size from a quarter pound to almost two pounds.

STRIPED BASS, BLUEFISH AND POLLOCK

The striped bass, native on the East Coast from Nova Scotia to Cape Hatteras and now native since its introduction on the West Coast from San Francisco to the state of Washington is one of the prime saltwater fishes for the fly fisherman. The bluefish, native only to the East Coast from Florida to Maine, and the pollock, found from Newfoundland down to Cape Cod, are in the same league.

All are common and available through fishing from the surf, jetty, inlets, and in the case of the striper—in brackish water. They all follow the bait schools. Fishing before the top of the tide and as it is falling are the best times, since it is then that baitfish are the most active. Casting and trolling are the techniques and big bucktails and streamers are used, as are jigs and fly and spinner combinations.

Stripers as heavy as forty pounds are taken readily on flies; bluefish of from three to ten pounds, and pollock from three to ten pounds are legion.

SNOOK AND TARPON

These two fish are residents of Florida and the Gulf Coast. They are found in brackish water, inlets, surf and off-shore to a certain extent. They go readily for flies cast into the tide when baitfish are plentiful and moving. Tarpon upwards of one hundred pounds are taken on flies and snook weighing forty pounds are not uncommon.

BONEFISH—FLORIDA AND THE BAHAMAS

This is perhaps the most glamorous of the saltwater fish. Bonefish demand the greatest talent of a fly fisherman and afford him the most sensational battle, despite their relatively small size. A six-pound bonefish is average-large, but when hooked he will streak out fifty yards of line in mere seconds. Fished for on the flats, they seem to have only one way to go and that is straight out, and they go with unbelievable power. While all manner of tackle is used, the fly rod is the most sporting way to fish for them.

Bonefish are easily spooked. They run in schools and travel to shallow waters in search of bottom bait such as crabs, shrimp and small baitfish and they nose into the mud for crustaceans.

Approaching a school of bonefish in the crystal clear waters— depth only two to ten feet—they are easily scared off by even the movement of the rod. A whole school can vanish in half a second, so the utmost care is taken throughout the approach, casting and presenting the fly.

To cast properly and over great distances the most powerful rod and balanced tackle is required. The reel must have at least one hundred yards of backing.

WEAKFISH, POMPANO, JACK CREVALLE AND OTHERS

Almost all species of the smaller saltwater fish that school or follow bait schools such as shrimp are top game fare for fly fishermen. For fishing success, it is mainly a matter of experimentation and learning their ways and habits.

10

~~~~~~

Notes on Setting Up a Fishing Trip

APART FROM THE enjoyment derived from the experience, itself, two elements are important towards enjoying a fishing trip to its fullest extent: adequate planning and provision for augmenting one's memory of the trip—this last perhaps most often overlooked. Without sufficient planning, a trip can be a bust and its memory something to be forgotten. If the trip is well planned, there is delight in the stage of planning and anticipation, great enjoyment in the fruits of such "labor" and a rich memory of the trip that will be in the angler's book for the rest of his life.

PLANNING

In the first stage of planning, there must be the dream of taking off from home to a far away fishing area, perhaps, and to fish for a

162

species that is entirely new to the angler. The country will be new, strange and exciting and the anticipation of catching different fish species will be something to look forward to, especially after sufficient study and research has been done. A dream like this can become a reality. For instance, the author dreamed of fishing for steelhead on the West Coast when he was just a youngster. Way back in Connecticut, he did his research and then one day finally got to fish for the steelies while in the military based at Ft. Lewis, Washington.

The various elements of planning a trip can be accomplished simultaneously or one at a time, depending on individual whim.

First, practical considerations. A trip is seen possible, financially and timewise. Where to go, how far, how long, what gear and what fish is the quarry?

Let's say the angler lives in New York City and desires to fish for smallmouth bass in Upper Maine. He's read of the chains of lakes there loaded with fighting bass plus the wonders of that state's great out-of-doors. But he doesn't just take off in the car with a rod, reel and tacklebox and head north—not if he's wise.

Let's start with the fish species. Smallmouth bass. There are many books that tell about this fish, biologically and from the sportsman's point of view. It is described briefly in another chapter. Learn about this fish, where he lives, how he lives, what he feeds on and when. Then study Chapter 7 on lake fishing and check the writings of other authors on smallmouth bass fishing, especially fly fishing and bass bug fishing. Write down their specifications on tackle requirements. Is the necessary tackle owned at the moment or does it have to be bought in order to go properly equipped? Will any outdoor camping equipment be needed?

To get the answers to these and other questions, routine research includes some writing and correspondence.

First, write to the State of Maine Travel and Publicity Department for a listing and description of the bass lakes and ponds that are the best bets for your trip. Then write the State of Maine Conservation Department for the latest dope on these lakes. Many of the states have monthly publications which detail their fishing waters and give the latest fishing conditions. Now, get a map and see just where these best lakes are. Note the names of principal towns nearby. Write to their Chambers of Commerce asking for promotion folders on nearby resorts, motels, outfitters and guides that cater to sportsmen. A very good source of this information is in the where-to-go section of national and regional sportsman's magazines, such as *Field and Stream, Outdoor Life* and *Sports Afield.* There will be many advertisements by guides, outfitters and fishing resorts. Write these people telling them your desires and asking about their facilities and prices. Inquire about what clothes to wear, what tackle to bring, the best time to come and whether they have guides, boats, motors and camping equipment for your use on the trip.

When boiled down to a specific area or lake, the next step may be to contact a local rod and gun club in the area, in order to find a fishing buddy for the trip, if one is wanted. The Federation of Fly Fishermen and Trout Unlimited have member clubs wherever there is good fly fishing and a letter to their headquarters will bring desired results.

When all this information is in and digested, the angler will begin to get the "feel" of the country, the people, the anglers, the type of fishing to be done, the kind of problems he'll run into, and he'll know a good deal about the fish he's after. Excitement builds up.

Reservations made well in advance are very important. With today's huge army of fishermen, good guides and good living quarters are not always available at the spur of the moment. It would be a waste of time and money to merely drive north, just hoping to find what is wanted.

As to tackle. The basic rods, reels and lines should be brought along from home. It is assumed that the angler knows how to rig, cast and fish this tackle like an expert. When the angler arrives at destination it is most probable that there will be special flies and rigs that are considered by the "locals" to be real fish-getters. Go well-equipped with a broad selection of flies and leaders, of course, but make it a point to visit the local tackle stores along the way and especially those in the vicinity of the fishing spot. Often these stores advertise in the mail-order sections of the big outdoor magazines. It doesn't hurt to buy a few flies from them even before the trip begins. If he can be found, a local fly-tier is a good man to know. He'll tie up some specials and may even take the angler fishing with him on his favorite lake or connecting stream.

GUIDES

A word now about the guide.

In the old days, a guide was a combination of a servant in the outdoors to handle all the details of camping, paddling the canoe or manning the boat. He also instructed his "sport" in the art of casting and gave generously of his fishing know-how, especially his knowledge of the lakes and waters where he'd grown up and lived all his life. His sharing of this background and experience made the trip a success or a failure. Guides of this kind are what made sport fishing the number one pastime of rich and poor alike.

When an angler visits strange country and fishes for a species with which he is unfamiliar, a guide is necessary. Even if the angler has fished all over the globe, the guide can save a lot of time trying to find the right lures, learning the proper ways to fish them, and most important, the guide will know just where the fish are in a given lake at a specific time.

But don't treat that guide as a servant. It is best to question and ask about his territory rather than try to impress upon him that the angler knows all about it and has merely hired him to paddle the canoe or man the outboard motor. If this becomes the relationship, that is all he *will* do. Make a friend of the guide, right from the start. Most of them are quite humble people and they love their lands and waters. They'll share all this with an angler who they respect and get to know as a good friend. They'll then take the angler to their pet, favorite spots.

MAPS AND CORRESPONDENCE

In addition to their knowledge, a certain amount of theoretical knowledge of water depths, temperatures and the depth lines of a lake are good to have along. A geodetic map of the territory is a great boon to supplement the combined knowledge of the angler and the guide. The guide may never have seen a geodetic map; his maps are usually in his head! Combine the two and the trip should have all the elements for success.

Planning a trout fishing excursion may demand a little more research. Suppose the angler resides in Virginia and wants to fish the fabulous Idaho-Montana country. The trout in Virginia and nearby Pennsylvania are one thing, but the trout in those big, broad Montana streams are something else again. They are both trout and the same gear is required to catch them, but from this point on, the angler is a stranger to the waters, the conditions, the best times for fly hatches, the actual natural insects that will be duplicated by artificial flies and the general run of stream tactics necessary for success. Outdoor camping and pack trips might be necessary. A guide must be contacted. This all means writing along the lines mentioned earlier plus some in-depth correspondence with local fly tiers, guides and outfitters. Here again, contacts with club members will yield much of value and perhaps new friendships. The brotherhood of anglers is a wondrous brotherhood and it doesn't matter if the angler is rich or poor, experienced or novice.

THE GEAR TO TAKE

As to the actual packing and selection of gear to be taken along, this author insists on a routine to follow in order not to forget anything. It is best to make a list of the requirements and then assemble all the gear owned, and if lacking, buy it with advice from a good fishing friend or a reliable fishing tackle dealer. Spend time with a tackle expert and one who knows something about fishing and living outdoors. Don't just go down to the local discount store and pick stuff at random. There is a lot of unnecessary junk there designed to sell at bargain prices, so don't be a chump!

TRIP DOSSIERS AND MEMORY AIDS

Keep a correspondence file. The trip to the same waters may be taken again in the future. Also, keep a diary and while on the trip make generous entries in it. Take some good pictures, not merely those of Joe holding up a dead fish. Make a record of the area through lake and water shots, the scenery and special features of the country, the guides and friends, their homes—even a picture of the local tackle shop or general store. Promise to send the locals some snaps of your trip with them and then keep the promise.

After many years of collecting such organized diaries and photo albums, the angler will have an invaluable memory file of his great experiences. I know of one angler who religiously kept such records and photos of all of his fishing trips; the results were eventually made into a book enjoyed by thousands of others.

Sooner or later the itch to repeat a particular trip will arise. Or, perhaps the angler will someday have a son who wants to fish the same waters. Maybe a friend will want to look over this collection of information for his own adventure. It is all there available to share. Yet even if not so used, when long winter evenings arrive, these trip dossiers refresh the memory, bring back pleasurable scenes and fond recollections of places, people and the so enriching quiet charm of the out-of-doors.

So, when it comes time to pack all the gear in the car, bring along the correspondence file. There will be entries to add while on the spot.

Yes, planning the trip and not skipping any details is fun and will contribute to a good experience, whether the trip be to familiar waters or to new far-away places.

11

~~~~~~~~~~~~~~~~~~~~~~~~~~~~~~~~~~~~~~

Some of Fly Fishing's Past

MEETING ANY TEN fly fishermen along a stream, the odds are great that at least nine of them will, in all likelihood, know little if anything on how American fly fishing tackle developed. The highlights of this usually overlooked history are reviewed in this chapter. On the other hand, should several of these same ten fishermen prove to be fly fishermen from way back, they probably will at least have heard of—if they haven't actually read some of the remarkable writings on the art of fly fishing, the highlights of which are here also reviewed.

The chief point, of course, is that since fly fishing's not exactly a relatively new fishing method, one can learn a very great deal from the literature which has evolved about the sport over the many years. Quite a few serious fly fishermen form their own reference libraries; some readers will therefore appreciate an overview of the angling literature extant. But first let's see how American tackle developed.

ON FLY FISHING TACKLE

The first important contribution to fly fishing in America by native craftsmen was shortening the fly rod from the European 10, 12 and 14-foot rods down to the 10, 8, and even six-foot size. This evolution came about gradually to fit American fishing conditions.

The conversion from horsehair lines to braided silk came next, and weight-forward lines, or bullet tapers were first designed in the U. S. Reels underwent mere detail refinements paralleling improvements made in England and France. The changes were dictated in part by the demands of the newer lines put on them. Leaders, made of gut until the coming of nylon from the U. S. and much later Perlon from Germany, was a next evolution along with fiberglass rods developed by American manufacturers. The manufacturing technique later was exported to England and Europe where glass rods have now all but replaced bamboo.

Historically, most researchers and authorities agree that the first rods to be built specifically for the trade in this country were by Charles E. Murphy of Newark, New Jersey in 1863. They were four-section rods sold through Andrew Clark and Co., of New York City, and later by L. H. Abbey who formed the well-known and first real tackle company—Abbey and Imbrie—in 1867. This operation preceded two other names credited with some of the first rods; Samuel Phillipi of Easton, Pennsylvania, who was also a gunmaker and who also developed the first multiplying reels, then later single-action fly reels carrying the brandname "Meek" in later years. The butts of his rods were of ash. But it was E. A. Green who is credited with the first all-bamboo split-cane rod, made in 1860.

This very small output, however, was hardly enough to justify saying that America was now producing its own. These men were known only in neighborhoods and if a person wanted to buy a fly rod, he still had to go to the "big city" and hope to find an importer, or some friend who owned an extra rod. So, for the next few years, trout fishing was limited to cane-pole fishing or the cutting of a streamside willow or alder pole—hardly the rig for the kind of dry fly fishing recommended by England's Halford!

Perhaps he was just a craftsman, not at all interested in the future market, or perhaps he did have a vision of what was to come. Anyway, Hirman Lewis Leonard, born January 23rd, 1831, was to become the man who really got things started. To this day the name Leonard on a fly rod, or on any rod is the most valuable label in the industry. The family moved to New York, then to Pennsylvania and later to Bangor, Maine where Leonard worked as a gunsmith and taxidermist, making his first personal fly rod in 1871. It was made of ash and lancewood. Meanwhile Tom Conway of New York had been making rods and Leonard decided to upstage him by making a better rod. Friends persuaded Conway to show his rod to Bradford and Anthony, a big sporting goods retailer in Boston. They took a rather dim view of it, however, not having been happy with any rods they'd seen, particularly those made of bamboo. When Leonard saw their rods of 4-strip bamboo, he remarked that he would do better and use 6-strip construction, and Leonard started looking for men who could learn the trade.

Soon the New York jobbers, Abbey and Imbrie took over Leonard's production. In 1877 he went into partnership with a Boston man named Kidder to finance the objectives. Wm. Mills, seeing a future in the Leonard product, bought out the investor's interest and Wm. Mills and Son became the final outlet. Wm. Mills, is the oldest tackle store in the United States. The son was Thomas B. Mills, whose son Arthur Mills, now retired, still carries on the family business, same name, with his son, Steven, running the operation.

Mills decided to move the factory·from Bangor to Central Valley, New York where it is today, though the old factory, a relic antique in itself, burned in the late Sixties, but was immediately rebuilt. Bamboo was by that time scarce, but fortunately, much of the stock on hand was saved.

Mills remained the fountainhead of talent in the rod business as W. Edwards, E. F. Payne, F. E. Thomas and Hiram Hawes built the team and then each left to go out on his own, fashioning rods that would be as famous as the original Leonard. In fact, they were all known as Leonard rods and their fame reached back even to England and Europe where they won first prizes at exhibitions in London, Vienna and at the Philadelphia World's Fair.

It was during this period that the switch from Calcutta to Tonkin cane was made, Tonkin being a far superior reed. The reason it is called cane is supposed to be because the old Chinese men walk with canes of bamboo!

The American improvement of quality was achieved by eliminating the rounded curves that the British formed on their assembled sections, thereby retaining the valuable outer thin edge of tough fibers, making the rod much stronger and having longer lasting qualities. Experiments with rods formed of four, five and seven bamboo strips were to come later.

About 1912 Abbey and Imbrie came out with the "steel vine" rod of only three strips. Even then the four-strip with its 90 degree angles was not good, yet it was reintroduced in the 1950's again by Edwards. This was a powerful rod, a backbreaker, but it was found wanting. Also in the late 1940's and early 1950's a Catskill rodmaker, Nat Uslan, produced a five-strip rod that threatened the popularity of the six-stripper. He used improvements in taper and combined taper with five-strip construction and a special bonding agent. His rods were excellent, fast, powerful and were made for all kinds of fishing except saltwater big game trolling. The experts consequently hovered around him like flies. Here was a seeming breakthrough in rod design. But, due to faulty business management and the scarcity of good quality Tonkin cane (because WW II closed off the supply), all rod manufacturers who did not have a large back-up supply almost went out of business. Uslan's business, because of this shortage, was short-lived and failed not because of the five-strip idea, but because of other complications. It is true that the five-strip construction with its wider edges did fatigue quicker than the six-strip, still it was nontheless a fine fly rod, especially for bigger fish such as bonefish and salmon.

Taper development was affected, too, by the invention of tapered lines. The seven-stage Hedge, developed by Marvin Hedge, a champion distance caster, started the line revolution in the 1940's. It all started with the so-called "circular" taper which, while as good as the uniform taper, was still lacking in drive and accuracy. Help from the European Charles Ritz and cooperation by John Alden Knight resulted in the design and construction of a parabolic rod, built by Jim Payne of the Payne Rod Company of New York. The chief customer was the famous sporting goods house, Abercrombie and Fitch of New York City.

Edward R. Hewitt developed the steep-taper rod action in the 1930's and 1940's with most of the action being in the upper third or quarter of the rod. It, too, was limited to short casts—long distance casting with it was impossible.

Steel rods of seam construction, then steel rods of tubular non-seam stepdown taper construction were perfected by True Temper in Cleveland, in the 1940's. These rods were light, powerful and seldom if ever took a "set." They were used hard by the experts yet seldom was there ever a broken or worn out rod. But steel, to the fishing expert, just did not have the "feel" of bamboo, though the steel tubular step-down taper did for thousands what glass would do in the future; it made it possible for more anglers to have a real "tool" for fishing. It could handle spinners, spoons, heavy bait rigs and also cast a brace of heavy weighted streamers a practical distance without fear of straining the rod, casting that to this day would be foolhardy using the classic bamboo rod.

In 1936, a new rodmaker came on the scene—Everett Garrison, inspired by a friend, Dr. George Parker Holden, trout fisherman, a man who made his own rods and also author of the classic books *The Idyle of the Split Bamboo,* and *Streamcraft.* Garrison caught the bug of rod making from Holden and started his own plant in 1933, working on the parabolic rod principle. But this rod, too, was found wanting, despite its ability to this day to deliver great distance with a minimum of muscle. It was a matter of compromising the true parabolic for other needs in the taper design.

One of the large rodmakers, tackle designers and marketers, the Charles F. Orvis Company of Manchester, Vermont worked with the new plastic Bakelite and experimented with impregnating this into the bamboo to strengthen the already strong fibers. This worked out well, though at first the rods were brittle, too brittle to stand overworking by anglers who delighted in their power and casting qualities. But today, the Orvis rod with its now perfected Bakelite is a favored rod in America. Orvis, a true quality house, makes the rod to perfection, using the finest guides and ferrules to be had.

In the next development the name Hewitt comes up again, for in the 1940's—once nylon had been placed on the market— Hewitt in his Neversink laboratory tried to blend in plastic resins with several strands of nylon. The resulting rod proved nothing as a performer, but the idea was good and it was later perfected in a working model by the Libby-Owens-Ford glass company. The Shakespeare Co., of Kalamazoo, Michigan took the lead then and produced the first tubular and solid-tapered glass rods. To this day their product is tops in glass along with others such as the Gordon, marketed through the Garcia Company. Now it was possible for many rodmakers to buy blanks. Special tapers had to be developed, of course, all over again since glass had different qualities from bamboo. Today, thanks to help from the entire rod industry, the competition in glass has produced refinements in taper and also in ferrules that flex properly with glass; this has been developed to near perfection. One West Coast company, Fenwick, has since even developed a non-ferrule joint. It is merely a spreading of glass cloth to form a ferrule out of the rod section, itself. This largely licks the ferrule-breaking problem and makes for a smoother casting rod.

One might think that advent of the glass rod spelled doom to the bamboo rodmakers, but they have held on through it all, most of them while staying in business, also making glass rods. With the supply of Tonkin cane improving right along, the bamboo rod will continue to be available to the die-hards and even the next generation of quality rod owners in rods of their own choice. Being a completely hand-made product, the bamboo rod, however, will always be costly by contrast to the glass one.

There is little new in the development of fly casting reels. About the only development was the advent of the automatic spring reel which retrieves line when a trigger on the reel is pressed, through activating a powerful spring. But this feature has been made now for over 30 years. The conventional single-action reel made in England has only been copied, although improved somewhat due to better metals, and the price held down by mass production. Japanese imports, copies of the Hardy, for example, sell for even less than half the Hardy price and they are quite serviceable.

The Pflueger Medalist, first produced in the 1930's and still one of the most popular fly reels in America, is a relatively low-cost reel but one with sufficient backbone to handle almost any chore. Its one drawback is that it is constructed with screws and these can come out at the worst time. An easy way to prevent this, however, is to cement the screws in. There have been some other innovations in reel manufacture, spurred largely by imports from Europe and Asia, the American way in tackle being to produce the same or similar reel, but at a mass-produced quantity and sometimes lesser quality to meet the stiff competition.

Mass distribution and its dramatic changes have definitely affected the tackle industry. Time was when sporting goods were a part of the local hardware store, or handled in a specialty shop operated by a fisherman and his wife who specialized in tackle, special flies and much hand repair or innovation. These still exist and many flourish despite the price-cutting chain stores having sporting goods departments. The latter can buy in mass quantities and sell for only one or two points over wholesale, thus cutting into the business of the specialized dealer who must—because of his overhead and personalized services—charge more for the same product. Also, fair trading seems to have all but disappeared from the selling scene and it is now strictly a price/slash business and highly competitive. Only a special trade is safe from this and this is with hand-made rods, special-order files and the like which only a few individual stores and some mail-order houses can handle successfully.

ON FLY FISHING LITERATURE

In all the annals of angling, there have been but a scant few books written about bait fishing, only two or three on spin-fishing but the art and sport of fly fishing has enjoyed the overwhelming total of more than 5000 titles since the early days when the sport was born and brought up in England.

This tells us something about fly fishing. It is one of the most unusual kinds of recreation. It must be to bring out all that talent in writing, gorgeous illustration and poetry. Some of the ancient books include, in each copy, actual feathers for tying the flies and even some actual tied flies. These books are priceless now and collectors pay thousands of dollars for them.

The history of fly fishing is contained and has been made to remain forever in these volumes. Fly fishing will always be the epitome of sport fishing because of its unique and continuing heritage.

Everything that has been learned is available in writings to the fly fishing student, serious angler and one who can appreciate the literature of fly fishing.

Mark Kerridge, founder member of the Orange County Fly Fishers and executive member of The Federation of Fly Fishers has recently given his priceless collection of thousands of books to the Patrons Collection at California State College at Fullerton, California. Mark collected these books over many years and the collection is worth thousands of dollars. Recently the author had the opportunity to browse through this magnificent collection in order to skim off the cream, a summary of which follows. This collection will live as a reminder of one man who cherished the art and its great literature.

The first American trout was exposed to the earliest emigrants near Cape Cod, for in that area the streams were "rich with trout" —sea-run brook trout. The first Thanksgiving was said to include in the menu, brook trout from the Indians, caught in nearby streams.

From this point on, the gradual development of sport fishing, particularly fly fishing, closely paralleled the discovery, exploration, and development of the land all the way to the Pacific Coast. Trout, bass, panfish, pike, pickerel—all the food and gamefishes were stock larder in all cook's stores.

Actually, fly fishing evolved then, from two distinct opposites; one the necessity to catch "a mess of fish" for the table, and in a very limited way, "angling" in the Old World tradition imported by a very few, the purists, the well-to-do "gentlemen of the rod" who fished for sport first, the larder being second in importance. The so-called "meat fishermen" caught fish in any way possible, from trot-lines, dynamite, nets, and simple cane or willow poles, string, bent pin and stone for a sinker, to the rods, reels and lines imported from Europe, mainly England. Flies were, until the 1800's, all imported. Few fishermen tied their own, or were in the business, nor were their patterns disclosed and cataloged until the 1850's.

Fly fishing as an art-sport, then, was severely limited to those who came over from England, were "gentlemen of the art" and looked upon their newfound virgin waters with delight. The brook trout was new to them, the brown did not arrive—imported from German stock—until 1880. The early settlers never saw a rain-bow trout until brave migrants reached the Rocky Mountains and the Pacific Coast in the 1750's.

Nor was there much early fishing literature except brief mentions in books printed in Europe concerning the forays of colonists into the great wilderness.

But, true to their calling, a few anglers have set down for us extensive works on the subject. Some anglers, from Walton on, seem to have been destined to be historians and teachers through word and art, and the American heritage in this respect grew by leaps and bounds, once a few of the population took time off from building a great new world to go fishing and then write about it.

In brief, the development of tackle was slow at first, following principles laid down in Europe, mainly in Britain. The development of rods, for example, was a continuation of British styles and techniques up until recent years, when innovations in materials and specific necessities, such as fly rods for saltwater gamefish came about. Even lines and their development followed the lead from overseas up until the 1950's, with the development of German-made plastics such as Perlon coming as it did soon after the perfection here of nylon. Gut leaders underwent little if any development through the century except for varied lengths and strengths for specific American fishing, that is, until nylon came along and completely revolutionized the leader for all time. Single-strand tapered leaders are still the latest and finest leader development of note. Hooks have remained stable items and though American firms do make and market very excellent hooks, the best still come from abroad. New styles have been developed, of course, mostly for bait fishing in salt water. Tackle accessories have changed little, with the exception of being made from better materials. The biggest contribution to angling in America has been the development and application of mass production techniques. Hand in hand with this has been the growth in sport fishing; there are annually over 40 million freshwater licenses issued and that does not, of course, number the hordes of saltwater anglers.

Starting piscatoria Americana was *Northern Memoirs,* written by Richard Frank in 1658, but not published until 1694. In it, he wrote extensively about fishing in America, primarily trout fishing. He may have been the first fly fisherman to sample the fishing fare of the New World and then write about it! Another early book was the Schuylkill Fishing Company's *History,* printed in Boston in 1830. Another volume written in 1739 was *A Discourse at Ammauskeeg Falls in the Fishing Season,* by Joseph Secombe and published in Boston in 1743.

From this most modest beginning, a hundred years were to pass before Dr. Jerome Smith, M.D., delayed his publication of the *Natural History of Fishes* in Massachusetts until 1833. In 1845 John Brown's *American Angling Guide* was written. The George Bethune's first American edition of *The Complete Angler* was published in New York in 1847. Horace Greeley, the great journalist, was quite a fisherman and in *Recollections of a Busy Life,* he tells of fishing for speckled trout (brook trout) on his farm in New Hampshire. Robert Barnwell Roosevelt wrote a number of books between 1879 and 1886 and in 1870, Seth Green and A. S. Collins wrote *Trout Culture* one of the earliest American books on this subject.

Then, William Cowper Prime's *I Go A-Fishing,* 1873, and Henry Van Dyke's *Fisherman's Luck,* 1899, were to become classics in the manner of typical European fishing literature, particularly in fly fishing. Charles Stevens' *Fly Fishing In Maine Lakes*, Boston, 1881 and Charles A. Farrar's publication *The Androscoggin Lakes*, 1887 and J. H. Keene's *Practical Fisherman* followed.

Again a temporary lull in angling literature until Charles Lanman, author of *Adventures in the Wilds of North America*, 1854, toured as far west as California.

Brown comments: "The artificial fly, so much used in England but of little favor in this country, not because it is not as good as bait, but because more skill is required in using it. While the more experienced sportsman from foreign parts will astonish the native by his dexterity in throwing the fly and killing almost incredible numbers of fish, where the unbeliever regards the fly as a useless article of tackle, but the skill necessary to success in this branch of the subject is not so great as the novice imagines. There are hundreds of good fly anglers and many who can throw a fly with the most experienced in Europe. The short one-handed rod, from ten to twelve feet in length is most common in use. Attached to the rod should be a reel containing thirty to fifty yards of hair, grass silk, or silk and hair line, the latter description should be used if it can be procured, tapering from the tenth of an inch almost to a point; to this should be attached a leader from one to two yards in length and finally your fly, on a light length of gut; if you wish to use two or three flies, place them on your leader or short gut about twenty-four inches apart."

Frank Forrester, the pen name of Henry William Herbert, published under Stringer and Townsend, N.Y. *Fish and Fishing* in 1850 and wrote about anglers extremely interested in the species of trout they found in the New World (brook trout). He mentions the Arctic Grayling as "Back's Grayling" taken from the waters of Great Slave Lake. He also mentions the varied salmon and trout of the Northwest. The brown trout, he concluded, was not a native of America except in the waters of the Eastern seaboard in New Brunswick, Canada and the Gulf of St. Lawrence waters. Forrester authored many books on fishing and the outdoors, including novels.

Perhaps the greatest milestone in American fishing literature came on the scene when Thaddeus Norris' *American Angler's Book* was published in Philadelphia in 1864.

An interesting quote: "The angler should not cast at random over the water but each portion of it should be carefully fished, the nearest, first."

Another writer of the 1800's, Genio C. Scott, wrote *Fishing in American Waters*, published in 1869 by Harper and Bros. In Part II of his book is found: "To cast a fly gracefully, so that it will fall in the right place like a snowflake, or light like a winged insect, requires practice. So soon as the angler learns to lay out thirty feet of line, straight, without a bend from the top of his rod, he may count himself a fly-fisher." While he does not specifically mention the dry fly, he speaks of trout rising and says: "And as a floating lure is better than a sinking one, the fly tiers prefer such floating hairs as those from hog's ears, seals, bears, the South American fox, otter, etc."

In *Western Trout Lore*, in 1883, G. O. Shields, better known as "Coquina", wrote "Rustling in the Rockies" which referred to the great fishing and later a chapter in the Rand McNally *American Game Fishes*, Chicago, 1892, "Trouts in Montana" was added to history. In conversation development, Shields was one of the first to broach the subject and was an ardent protectionist visualizing the effects of the wanton slaughter of both game and fish.

After the rush for gold to California, John L. King's *Trouting on the Brule River*, 1879 and Charles Hallock's *The Fishing Tourist*, 1873 recounted the then blooming sport of angling, especially for trout.

But the Eastern section of the country was still to spawn a great fund of American literature and authors on fishing—from New England, the New York Adirondacks, the Catskills (which still produce top angling writers) and the Blue Ridge Mountains. All books of this period were published in New York or Boston, later in Cincinnati and Chicago.

One of the landmarks was Professor George B. Goode's *The Fisheries of the U. S.* and the classic *Game Fishes of the United States*, (1878–1880). His comment on fly fishing for catfish: "A spice of danger attends its capture and perhaps the excitement of taking one of them off the hook atones in part for its lack of gameness in the water, for a well constituted catfish always gorges the hood and its spines, always erect, inflict powerful wounds."

In his book *Fishing With the Fly*, published in 1883, Charles F. Orvis, whose works have contributed to both American angling literature and better tackle includes contributions by a large group of then popular angling writers and helps fishing history by their inclusion. Charles Hallock, Henry P. Wells, Seth Green, W. C. Prime, R. B. Roosevelt, Dr. James Henshall, remembered for his book on the black bass, and Dr. C. J. Kenworthy.

The year 1892 saw the publication of Rand McNally's *The American Angler*, with an introduction by A. N. Chaney including chapters on the brook trout, trouting in Nipigon, The Rocky Mountain Trout and The Grayling. The last chapter covers William C. Harris's fishing experiences on the Gallatin in Montana for grayling, using a brown hackle and a coachman fly and having such fine fishing he was "sated."

The classic book, *Favorite Flies and their Histories* by Mary Orvis Marbury, Boston & New York, 1892, is a wildlife dictionary with excellent color plates of favorite flies and to this day remains the best contribution to fly fishing flies and the art of tying them.

One of the most romantic fly tying anglers of the 1800's was the more recently famous Theodore Gordon, after whom the Theodore Gordon Fly Fishers, a unique fly fishing brotherhood, take their name. Legend reports that he was a sick man who came to live in the Catskill Mountains, the birthplace of classical trout fly fishing in the U. S. He was an avid fly tier and experimenter, tying flies and assisting many then prominent anglers who came up from New York. The Quill Gordon fly, imitating one of the first early Mayflies to hatch on the Catskill streams, was one of many flies he designed.

The "American Halford"—here Gordon went one step further by developing a dry fly for American waters, but at the same time he discouraged the fact that the dry fly was the only method to use.

Meanwhile, on the Pacific Coast, angling was becoming a sport and Professor Louis Agaissiz, a Harvard professor and zoologist, wrote *On Extraordinary Fishes of California*, published in New

Haven Conn., in 1853. Stewart Edward White came to California in 1903 to fish for the hardly known golden trout of the High Sierras. He was afraid that the golden would become extinct from over-fishing and wrong use of the watershed that harbored this species above the 10,000 foot elevation, and so told President Theodore Roosevelt about it, the President then taking steps to institute a study by the Bureau of Fisheries under the direction of Burton Warren Evermann. In 1904, White wrote a chapter on the golden trout in *The Outlook.*

Another early western writer was David Starr Jordan, who in 1882 began his studies of the American fishes (*Fishes of North America*). With his close associate, Barton Warren Evermann, he composed a four-volume study entitled *Fishes of Middle and North America.* His magnificent study of American fishes entitled *American Food and Game Fish* with color plates was published in 1902 by Doubleday, Page, N.Y. He also wrote *Trout and Salmon of the Pacific Coast* in 1906, and *A Guide to Fishes* in 1905. His climax writing was the first detailed study of the golden trout of the High Sierras in 1905, printed in the U. S. Bulletin of Fisheries, consisting of 51 pages and three color plates of the golden trout. Evermann was later director of museums for the California Academy of Sciences, and Jordan, Chancellor of Stanford University.

From 1900 on, the list of angling writers and experts has grown in magnitude, but three names stand out for the first part of this period. The wealthy sportsman, George M. L. LaBranche, who many of the present-day angling fraternity of the Angler's Club of New York remember well, published his *The Dry Fly in Fast Water* (as opposed to the conventional English chalk stream context) in 1914, and as Emlin Gill once said: "LaBranche is America's top notch fly fisherman."

George Fredrick Holder, in 1908 wrote extensively about saltwater fishing and included fly fishing, probably under the heading of trolling. His freshwater writing, especially for trout and fly fishing, was extensive and he was a great contributor to California's status in fly fishing.

The year of 1923 was one of historical interest when W. H. Shelby, then a director of the Bulletin of The California Fisheries Department, maintained what was probably one of the earliest commercial fish hatcheries in the West. In 1923 the state completed arrangements to trade a million Loch Leven brown trout eggs for a million brook trout eggs, and was successful in developing a pure stock of brook trout directly from the Eastern strain.

Louis Rhead, a New Yorker, following along in English Ronald's tradition, wrote of his experiment in insect classification and fly patterns. He was also an artist, illustrating his two books, *The Speckled Trout*, N. Y. 1902, and *Fisherman's Lures and Game Fish*, Ford, N.Y., 1920.

Back East, high in the Catskills and on the banks of the Neversink, over the hill from the famed Beaverkill, Edward R. Hewitt, a wealthy mining engineer and industrialist-inventor, owned a long stretch of this famous river. Not only was he a fine writer-experimenter, but the father of much of American technique. He invented the bi-visible dry fly, one of all hackle, no wings, but with a couple of turns of white at the front to enable the angler to see the fly under poor light conditions. Another fly that was found to bring impressive results was his Neversink Skater, an imitation of the Mayfly spinner as well as the spider. His books, *Better Trout Streams* and *Telling on the Trout* were published in the early Thirties.

Eugene V. Connett brought the flavor of factual angling literature on a par with anything from England to his writing and later to his publishing firm, The Derrydale Press. Connett's *My Friend the Trout* and *Any Luck* are classics. *Random Casts*, illustrated by William Shaldach, top-flight American fishing artist, did the illustrations for this and many other of the now untouchable Derrydale editions.

In the East certain gentlemen of the fly rod were becoming interested in forming a new cult of fly fishing stressing the use of natural flies and their imitations. Following along the lines laid down by Skues and Halford, was Theodore Gordon with his naturals, followed by Preston Jennings *A Book of Trout Flies* in which he cataloged the general types of Mayflies, caddis flies and stone flies of New York and Pennsylvania streams and tied special patterns to imitate them. Dan Cahill, a New York state fly tier, was credited with the invention of the Cahill flies, both light, dark and quill (patterns). The Hendrickson, in that same era, was named after Albert Everett Hendrickson of Scarsdale, N.Y., a prominent angler and member of the Angler's Club of New York.

The more scientific approach to the subject was followed by the writings in both magazines and books of James Leisenring of Pennsylvania, Ray Bergman, fishing editor of *Outdoor Life* magazine and author of several books, the most famous and today still a best seller, *Trout*, published by Alfred Knopf, 1939.

On the West Coast, not to be outdone, was a great angler, Claude Kreider, author of *Steelhead*, 1948, and *The Bamboo Rod*, 1951. He knew the West and western trout better than most writers of even the present day and wrote with authority and simple direct style. Another back country author and explorer of the high altitudes was Charlie McDermond, author of *Waters of the Golden Trout Country*, 1946, and *Yosemite and Kings Canyon Trout*, 1947.

Dr. Paul R. Needham, Ph.D., aquatic biologist, U. S. Bureau of Fishing and ichthyologist for the University of California wrote back in 1938 the book now famous, *Trout Streams*, published by Comstock in Ithaca, N.Y. Needham contributed in great amount to the development of knowledge of fish, fisheries and the natural foods of the trout, in particular.

Back in Pennsylvania, one of the America's greatest, often referred to as the American Halford, was Charles M. Wetzel who authored *The Art of Fly Tying, American Fishing Books*, and his best, *Practical Fly Fishing*. The climax of his writing was *Trout Flies, Naturals and Their Imitations*, a book still referred to by the experts on the technical side of developing natural fly imitations and representing the entomologists' approach to the art. Vincent Marinaro's *A Dry Fly Code*, 1950, N. Y., is a pillar in this category, too.

Art Flick, a follower of Jennings, and in all modesty, this author as well, have contributed much in magazines on the specific art of wet fly and nymph "naturals." There's also my book, *How to Take Trout on Wet Flies and Nymphs*, Little Brown, 1950, representing the first nymph-insect technique-strategy book. Another contribution is *Tactics on Trout*, Knopf, 1969.

Forward to the present day, the list of knowledgeable writers seems almost unending, many contributing to angling lore through magazine articles. Such a list would include Ernie Schweibert, John McDonald, Joe Brooks, Joe Bates, and the renowned Lee Wulff, *Atlantic Salmon*, N. Y., 1968; Al McClane, fishing editor of *Field and Stream* and author of *The Fisherman's Encyclopedia*, Arnold Gingrich, editor of *Esquire* magazine, author of *The Well Tempered Angler*, Knopf, 1965. Many others deserve mention, Lee Hidy, Jim Quick, William F. Blades, Donald DuBois, Sid Gordon, Dr. Carl Richards and Douglas Swisher of Rockford, Illinois for their latest no-hackle fly contributions based on experiences in the AuSable river of Michigan; Charles Fox, author of *The Wonderful World of Trout*, 1953 and *Rising Trout*, 1967.

In Western Canada, Roderick Haig-Brown has carved a special niche in American angling. A British-born angler, he settled in British Columbia and has produced several books that have become classics, *The Western Angler*, N. Y., 1939, first issued by Derrydale Press, a four-book series, and his classic *Return To the River*, Crown, N. Y., 1941.

No doubt there are many others deserving mention.

12

Conservation and the
FFF

THE UNITED STATES has gone through three phases of development in terms of wildlife and natural resources; those of discovery, settlement and development. This last, development, has involved harsh devastation from unwise use of natural resources. As man moved West, the natural resources were all but ruined on all fronts and strong conservation measures were late in coming and even later in repairing the damages of times past. The West is still partly wild and somewhat untouched, though recent years have shown harsh inroads into the wilds. Today conservation and the new word "ecology" have brought the plight of natural resources to the public eye and plans and laws are being developed to protect what is left and, hopefully, to retrieve what has been lost.

CONSERVATION

In the field of outdoor sport, the conservation departments of the federal, state and local governments have cooperated in a mass program of clean-up and conservation plus the development of more natural lakes and rivers for sport fishing. Added to this the work of individual conservation organizations and associations such as The Izaak Walton League, the National Audubon Society, Trout Unlimited, The Federation of Fly Fishers (International) and state groups such as California Trout, most all of which have banded together through a large membership to join in to make our rivers "wild rivers"—not subject to dams and other uses. The demand for power, flood control, irrigation and drinking water have and will seriously threaten the natural watersheds all over the country and the need is to use these waters for the benefit of all.

America's growing pains are still in evidence. The millions of sport fishermen and nature lovers, not to mention those with intense cultural, aesthetic and—let's face it—commercial interests in terms of vacation and recreation businesses, are competing to "capture" the remaining land.

Still, the future of outdoor sport and recreation looks brighter now than ever before since the public has become alarmed at the inroads of civilization via real estate developers, sprawling suburbia and the demand for timber, water and other natural resources. A balance of demand and right use will emerge as a public policy and it will have to be rigidly enforced with the reclaiming of barren lands, development of watersheds, forests and plains for man's benefit, both recreational and commercial.

The main cost of conservation and law enforcement through the federal government and the states is financed thru sport license fees and the Pittman-Robertson Act taxes on sporting equipment which sportsmen voted for this purpose of state use after national collection.

The press of the country, including the national and regional sporting magazines, conservation department publications, college and scientific papers continually promotes wise use of resources and reports developments on the scientific front which will aid the cause.

The Outdoor Writers Association of America comprises the news media columnists of most of the papers, magazines, book authors, illustrators and publishers. They in large part are responsible for public attention to the important matter of getting everyone to know and live with this planet in peace.

Anglers, too, have adopted voluntary restrictions, particularly in trout fishing by promoting fly-fishing-only, lower creel limits and the use of barbless hooks. It is to be hoped that trout fishing will become a true art form similar to that enjoyed on the private waters of Europe, but with the democratic spirit rather than a wealth-limited purism devotion.

FEDERATION OF FLY FISHERMEN (FFF)

It is difficult to say exactly how the idea that there should be some kind of national fly fishing organization first originated. It seems to have sprung up somewhat spontaneously as various clubs and individuals across the country realized that unity and strength might be built through such an association and that there was no other organization with which fly fishermen could affiliate to the same ends.

To mention a few specific names, we should recognize the early impetus from the Theodore Gordon Flyfishers, New York, and from individual members of that club, especially Gene Anderegg, Theodore Rogowski and Lee Wulff. Interest was also manifest from McKensie Flyfishers, Oregon under the leadership of Bill Nelson, and Fly Fishermen For Conservation, Fresno, Calif., with E. J. Strickland participating in the early discussions.

It is easier to pinpoint the first overt move, in September, 1964, when the then-young and eager McKensie club sent a task force consisting of Bill Nelson, Stanley Walters and Riley Woodford to a national meeting at Aspen, Colorado. This group met Gene Anderegg at their meeting and in an extended discussion a plan for a national organization was worked out. McKensie volunteered to host the national meeting which was considered necessary.

Returning home, McKensie set to work vigorously, publicizing the proposed meeting and invited all known clubs and individual fishermen to join in the effort. Their work was so successful that representatives of 12 clubs together with some 200 individual fishermen met on June 18–20, 1965 at the beautiful Country Squire Motel, Eugene, Oregon, for the first introductory conclave.

McKensie, with the assistance of Anderegg, lined up a program which included such nationally-known figures as Lee Wulff, Ed Zern and Ted Trueblood. Among others contributing individually were Lewis Bell, Everett, Washington, Lewis Garlick, U. S. Fish and Wildlife, Rick Miller, Seattle, Washington, David Hurn, Vancouver, B. C., Enos Bradner, Seattle, and Ashley Hewitt, Pasadena, son of the famous E. R. Hewitt.

Panel discussions were provided on appropriate subjects with Richard Thompson, U. S. Fish and Wildlife, S. B. Smith, Fisheries Management, British Columbia, V. S. (Pete) Hidy, Portland, Oregon, Don Myrick, Medford, Oregon, Dr. John Rayner, Oregon Game Commission, and Mike Starr, Eugene, being prominent partipants in these panels.

And so FFF was born!

The Federation of Fly Fishermen (International) is an affiliation of fly fishing clubs, 90 strong and growing. Organized in 1955, the Federation today represents some 25,000 club members in the United States, Canada, New Zealand and France. Its purpose is to preserve the past, promote the present and protect the future of fly fishing as a sport. To achieve these basic goals, it works at the local level through affiliated clubs and nationally through an elected board of directors.

The activities of the Federation reflect a dual interest in protecting water resources and in promoting fly fishing as a sport. On the conservation front, the Federation is active in CASE (The Committee on the Atlantic Salmon Emergency) and the North American Atlantic Salmon Council.

It has been in the forefront of conservation efforts to stop the Tocks Island Dam on the Delaware and the Hells Canyon and Teton Dams in Idaho. And it has been a leader in the fight to preserve the Klamath, Trinity and Eel Rivers in California. Through position papers on stream channelization, estuary conservation, wild trout programs and logging practices, the Federation further supports sound water resources and conservation at the national level. And, equally important, Federation clubs supported by the national organization work actively to protect local water resources and to improve stream management practices in their own areas.

Affiliation with the Federation, through a club or individually as an associate member, offers anglers a chance to take part in a program that mixes conservation and the pleasures of fly fishing. The Federation has established a stream monitoring system called the Water Watchers Program through which local clubs and individuals may take a personal part in protecting the waters in which they fish.

Another program developed by Federation members is available for stream bed plantings of trout eggs. An annual national conclave, an audio-visual library, fly casting kits, casting games, fly tying programs, a quarterly bulletin and a magazine called *The Fly Fisher* are other examples of what the Federation offers its members to further their enjoyment of fly fishing.

Information about membership in the Federation of Fly Fishermen and its programs is available from the Membership Service Office, 15513 Haas Ave., Gardenia, Calif., 90249.

Notes

IN THE MATTER of developing fly patterns and styles in the U.S., refer to the various book authors mentioned (see next page). Most, if not all of them, have contributed importantly in pattern design and fishing knowledge; then check individual fly tiers in specific locations and on popular streams, such as Harry Darbee on the Beaverkill in N. Y. State, and countless others who design flies for their specific fishing locale. The scene keeps changing all the time in development of fly patterns, styles and manner of fishing.

In education, several American universities such as Pennsylvania State, Montana State, California State and several others including high schools now have credited full-term courses in fly tying, fly and all-method fishing, plus a smattering of stream entomology and the history of angling. The Fenwick Tackle Company, makers of fine rods, also have a curricula of fly fishing with seasonal schools in ten states that last for as long as two weeks where the students get the full education to make them competent fly fishermen. Add to this the very active fishing clubs that have their own instructional sessions in fly tying, rod building and field trips and it is plain that fishing education with overtones of conservation emphasis are helping to shape the future of angling in America.

In the late 1960's the Orvis Rod Company of Manchester, Vermont started a fly fishing museum which is now growing steadily. Books and ancient fishing tackle, including gear owned by famous anglers is there to see and admire. Culturally, then, fly fishing is entering a new and expanding future.

SUGGESTED ADDITIONAL READINGS

A MODERN DRY FLY CODE Vincent Marinaro, Crown
NEW STREAMSIDE GUIDE Art Flick, Crown
MATCHING THE HATCH Ernest Schwiebert, Jr. Crown
FISHING THE NYMPH Jim Quick, Barnes
PRACTICAL STEELHEAD FISHING James Freeman, Barnes
COMPLETE BOOK OF FLY FISHING Joe Brooks, Harper & Row
TROUT Ray Bergman, Knopf
TACTICS ON TROUT Ray Ovington, Knopf
SALT WATER FLY FISHING George X. Sand, Knopf
THE ATLANTIC SALMON Lee Wulff, Barnes
SELECTIVE TROUT Swisher-Richards, Crown
WET FLIES, NYMPHS AND TROUT Ray Ovington, Freshet
LORE OF THE DRY FLY Ray Ovington, Freshet
CURRENTS AND EDDIES Wm. Shaldach, Freshet
LURE AND LORE OF TROUT FISHING Alvin Grove, Jr., Freshet
THE FLY AND THE FISH John Atherton, Freshet
STREAMER FLY TYING AND FISHING Joe Bates, Crown
McCLANE'S STANDARD FISHING ENCLYCOPEDIA Wm. Wise

THE ART OF TYING THE WET FLY AND FISHING THE
FLYMPH Leisenring and Hidy, Crown